POEMS OF CATUL

52
42
38
53
5
4 - Fabullus
17 - Nympi.
34
60
58
33
36
51

Revised already	still to do
1	13/34
3	45
7	46
8	51
10	64/70
11	72
12	84
31	85
	101

POEMS OF CATULLUS

CHOSEN AND EDITED BY
G.A. WILLIAMSON
FORMERLY SENIOR CLASSICAL MASTER,
NORWICH SCHOOL

PUBLISHED BY BRISTOL CLASSICAL PRESS
GENERAL EDITOR: JOHN H. BETTS
(BY ARRANGEMENT WITH BELL & HYMAN LTD)

Cover illustration: from an engraved carnelian gem of the
first century BC; Ashmolean Museum, Oxford.
[Drawing by Jean Bees]

First published by G. Bell & Sons Ltd in 1969

Reprinted by permission of Bell & Hyman Ltd
1986, 1994, by
Bristol Classical Press
an imprint of
Gerald Duckworth & Co. Ltd
The Old Piano Factory
48 Hoxton Square, London N1 6PB

© Bell & Hyman Ltd, 1969

All rights reserved. No part of this publication
may be reproduced, stored in a retrieval system, or
transmitted, in any form or by any means, electronic,
mechanical, photocopying, recording or otherwise,
without the prior permission of the publisher.

A catalogue record for this book is available
from the British Library

ISBN 0-86292-211-9

Available in USA and Canada from:
Focus Information Group
PO Box 369
Newburyport
MA 01950

Printed in Great Britain by
Booksprint, Bristol

PREFACE

THERE is no Latin author more suitable for Sixth Form study than Catullus. The variety of his subject-matter, the range of his emotions, the originality of his ideas, and the superb quality of his verse combine to make the reading of his poems a delight to both teacher and taught. It is of course impossible to tackle the whole of his writings and a selection must be made. The present volume includes almost every poem that can be read and explained without embarrassment, and excisions have been kept to a minimum. As the order in which the poems appear in the manuscripts is notoriously unsatisfactory, those selected have been rearranged in groups according to their subject-matter, and within those groups an attempt has been made to place them in an intelligible order. The longer poems have been grouped together at the end. If time is too short for the whole selection to be read, one or more of these longer poems can be omitted, for example no. 61, which the poet left unrevised, no. 64, which is not an original poem but a translation, and no. 66, which is by far the longest; or no. 66 can be shortened by taking the picture out of its frame, in other words, by reading only lines 47–267. The conventional numbering of the poems is given in Roman numerals at the end of each poem.

The Introduction has been limited to those facts which should be known to the student before he begins to read the poems; less important matters have been relegated to the Notes and Appendices. The notes have been kept brief—long explanations are rarely studied—their purpose being to enable the reader to understand and appreciate the poems rather than to extend his knowledge. Since Catullus employs many words which school pupils are not likely to have met before, the provision of a select vocabulary, besides enabling the notes to be kept short, will save much wearisome hunting in a dictionary and allow more time for studying the poems themselves, while leaving no excuse for guesswork; but as no one should attempt such an author unless the words in common use are already stored in his memory, I have included only such words as are likely to give trouble.

The text, printed by permission of the Clarendon Press, is that edited by Professor Mynors for the Oxford Classical Texts. Except for the omissions and renumbering already referred to and for the provision of English titles, no alteration has been made. Students unused to the disuse of the letter *v* may find this puzzling at first, but will soon get used to it. After all, it is quite illogical to dispense with *j* and retain *v*, and the Roman poets regarded the vocalic and consonantal values of *u* as interchangeable, making *genua* and *tenuis* dissyllabic and *silua* and *soluit* trisyllabic whenever it suited their convenience.

In the Notes I have inevitably drawn heavily on the full and scholarly edition of the poems by Professor Fordyce, whom I mention by name over and over again in acknowledgment of my debt. I have made use also of Simpson's edition (Macmillan), which has done noble service for nearly a century, and have been glad to quote a number of words and phrases from Cornish's translation in the Loeb Classical Library.

Norwich
November, 1968

G. A. W.

CONTENTS

	PAGE
INTRODUCTION	1

THE POEMS

Part One—Shorter Poems

I FRIENDS AND FOES
- (a) Good friends — 15
- (b) Disappointing friends — 18
- (c) Foes — 20
- (d) Friends and foes contrasted — 21
- (e) Objectionable people — 22

II POETS AND ORATORS
- (a) Good — 24
- (b) Bad — 25
- (c) Good and bad contrasted — 28

III THE LOST BROTHER — 30

IV HOME — 32

V LESBIA
- (a) Happy days — 34
- (b) Doubt — 37
- (c) The break — 39
- (d) Resignation — 40

VI VARIED THEMES — 43

Part Two—Longer Poems

'Too Sad to Write' (ii) — 49
'Marriage Song' (i) — 54
'Marriage Song' (ii) — 60
'Berenice's Lock' — 63
'Attis' — 66
'The Marriage of Peleus and Thetis' — 69

vii

NOTES 83
APPENDICES
    THE MANUSCRIPTS 173
    THE METRES 175
SELECT VOCABULARY 180

MAPS

The Home Country   3
The Wider World   9

INTRODUCTION

1 THE MAN AND HIS BOOK

There are some writers whose subject-matter lies outside themselves, who are fascinated by wars and sieges, plagues and calamities, voyages and romances, in which they have taken no part; by tragic events which have in no way affected themselves; by the common lot of all mankind; or by natural phenomena and philosophical systems of thought. These things they see, it is true, with their own eyes and feel according to their own sensibility, but only indirectly do they write about themselves. Another man could handle the same themes, or they themselves could have handled them equally well if they had been born in another time and place, so that our appreciation of their work does not greatly depend on our knowledge of their personal history.

Others there are whose minds are filled with their own experiences, their relations with other individuals, their joys and sorrows, their loves and hates, hopes and disappointments. Their writings can be understood only in the light of their own personalities and their own adventures. The more we know about such writers the more we can appreciate their writings; and conversely the more we study their writings the more we can learn about the writers. The men are inseparable from their works.

It happened that the Roman Republic produced two contemporary poets who illustrate this contrast to an extreme degree, Lucretius and Catullus. In the *De Rerum Natura* we catch glimpses of the moral fervour and human sympathies of Lucretius; but our understanding of that great poem, in the main an exposition in verse of the doctrines of Epicurus, does not depend on knowledge of the author's life and situation. Catullus, on the other hand, reflects in almost every line his ever-changing emotions and the incidents of his brief but stormy career. He does not generalise—all his poems are about individual persons and places, sharply distinguished and contrasted, arousing in him the most intense emotional reaction. It is impossible to separate the poems from the poet, or the poet from his time and place, his surroundings and the circle in which he moved; and it is from the poems that we derive most of our knowledge of the poet: there has surely never been a writer who by his poetry has enabled his readers to know him so intimately.

What can we learn about him from other sources? Very little. We have a statement written by St. Jerome five centuries after the poet's time, from which we gather that he was born in Verona in 87 B.C. and died in 58 in his thirtieth year. The second date is certainly wrong, for Catullus alludes in different poems to the second consulship of Pompey and to Pompey's Portico, and three times to Caesar's invasion of Britain; so that he must have been alive in 55 B.C. There seem, however, to be no allusions to events of the following year; so it is generally agreed that he died in 54, only a few months after his elder contemporary, Lucretius. If, as Jerome states, he was then twenty-nine, he must have been born in 83 or late in 84; and Palmer is probably right in suggesting that Jerome, who measured time by Olympiads, made a mistake of one Olympiad (four years) in each case.

Verona was a city of Cisalpine Gaul, a district inhabited by a mixture of Celts and Italians with a character of their own, much more lively and sensitive than that of the Romans. We must beware of thinking that poets who wrote in Latin were Romans: with the notable exception of Lucretius Rome did not give birth to poets. But Rome was a magnet that attracted all the poets to herself. However loudly they sang the praises of the countryside they inevitably settled in Rome. Catullus was no exception: at an

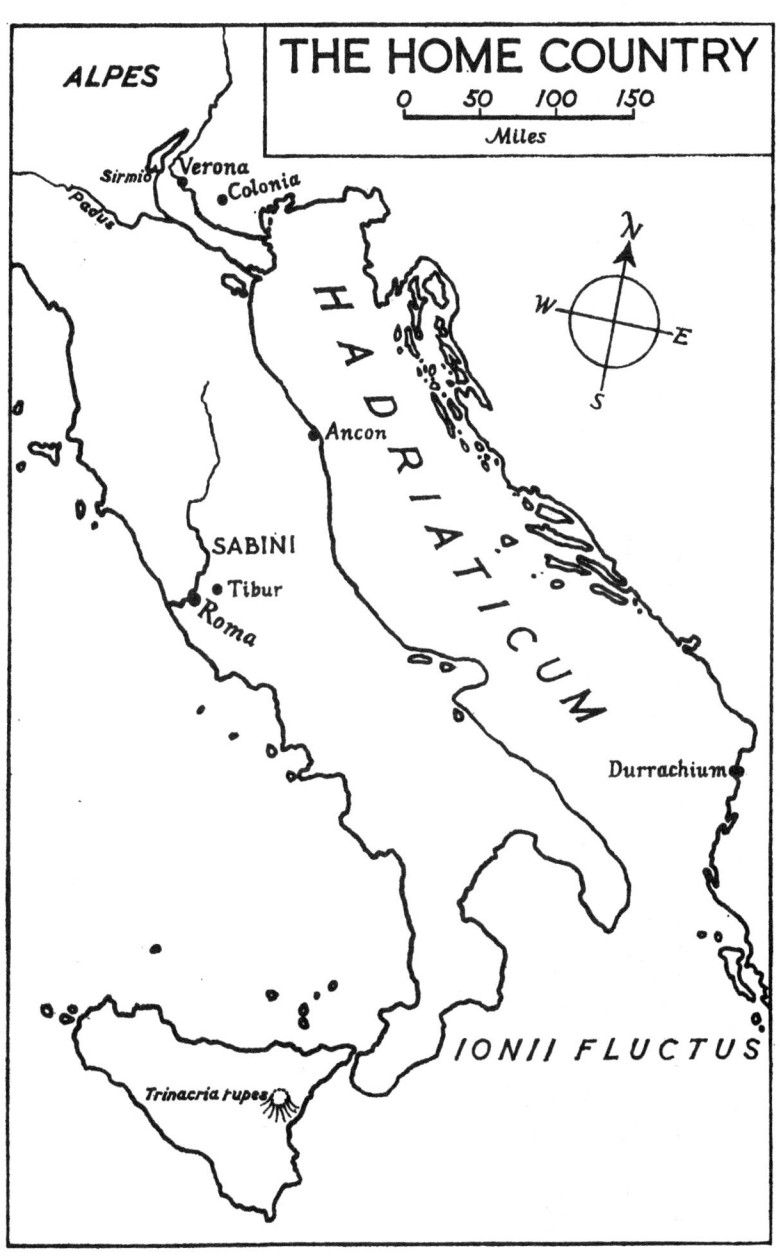

early age he migrated to the capital, and there plunged into the society of a group of young men, many of them poets and orators, highly intellectual, highly original, utterly sophisticated, and extremely clever, who revered neither the old Roman virtues nor the established literary conventions, and had no respect for the State religion; who lived entirely in the present and desired little beyond the pleasures of the moment, and regarded recognised moral principles as senseless taboos. There was no vice known to man which they did not talk about and in many cases practise. We shall meet many of these young men in the pages of this book.

It is therefore not surprising that Catullus, the most susceptible of men, soon became entangled in an affair with a married woman, an affair which was to cause him an intensity of joy and anguish of which his contemporaries were probably incapable, and to provoke him to write poem after poem, whose power to move and entrance his readers is as strong today as when they were composed. He calls the lady Lesbia. We know that her real name was Clodia, and it is almost certain that she was the sister of the notorious tribune, Clodius Pulcer, and the wife of Metellus Celer. The affair began before the death of Metellus in 59 B.C.—poisoned, it was whispered, by his charming wife—and was later wrecked by the multiplicity of Lesbia's amours, though for a considerable time Catullus clung to the hope of reconciliation.

Like his friends Catullus was a spendthrift, and it was in the expectation of lining his purse with something better than cobwebs that in 57 B.C. he set off for Bithynia in the train of the propraetor Gaius Memmius, a doubtful character to whom Lucretius had surprisingly addressed his mighty poem. It was the custom of Roman governors in Republican times to make it easy for their hangers-on to plunder the unfortunate subjects of Rome; but Catullus did not find his patron at all helpful, and he returned to Rome as poor as ever. On the way he visited the grave of his brother in the Troad, which moved him to write one of the most touching of his poems. The rest of his short life he seems to have passed in Rome, except for occasional visits to his birthplace and to his villas at Tibur and Sirmio.

For a man who died so young his output of poetry was considerable. Some poems are lost altogether, some are fragmentary; but those that have survived contain over two thousand lines, nearly as many as the four *Georgics* of Vergil. In the volume that has come down to us the poems are in no intelligible order. They are, it is true, arranged in three groups—first, fifty-seven* short poems in various metres of which the Hendecasyllabic is by far the commonest; then four longer poems, of which two are in hexameters; and finally fifty-two Elegiac poems, ranging in length from two lines to a hundred and sixty, the five longest being put nearest to the middle group. But within these groups there is no arrangement by subject-matter and no correspondence with the sequence of composition. We jump without warning from grave to gay, from sublime to obscene, from final disillusionment to youthful confidence. The farewell to Lesbia, written at the very end of the heartbroken poet's life, is placed almost at the beginning. It is impossible to believe that Catullus intended his poems to be read in such an order, and—at least for readers making his acquaintance for the first time—such an arrangement as is adopted in the present selection has obvious advantages.

2 His Debt to his Predecessors

Horace tells us frankly that poetry owes more to study than to inspiration, and it is certain that he and his fellow-Augustans spent very many hours in their libraries poring over the writings of the Greeks, from whom they took over both themes and poetical technique. The previous generation of Roman poets had done the same. There were of course Latin models such as the epic poetry of Ennius, which appealed to the austere mind of Lucretius. But to Catullus

---

* Not counting nos. 18–20, which are condemned as spurious.

and the group of ardent and rebellious young writers to which he belonged—the *noui poetae* of Cicero—Greek models had far more to offer. They were lighter, cleverer, more cultivated, more diverse in subject-matter and in the wonderful variety of metres employed. The agile mind and volatile spirit of Catullus, together with his far from puritan temperament, found in them just what he needed: and he had the ability to make Greek models and Greek methods his servants, not his masters, and to use them as a means of expressing Roman ideas and his own passionate feelings.

To us Greek poetry means the great dramas of the Fifth Century before Christ and the epic and lyrical writings of a still earlier date: to the Romans of Catullus' time it often meant the works of the more recent and very popular Alexandrian School. But Catullus himself was far too original to be a mere imitator of any exemplars, and his debt to the Alexandrians must not be exaggerated. As Ellis remarks, 'Virgil and Propertius show far clearer proofs of direct and conscious imitation.' Catullus, when he was too sad to produce an original poem, translated Callimachus; but he translated Sappho as well. He borrowed from other Alexandrian poets, especially Theocritus and Apollonius; but he borrowed twice as often from earlier writers, most notably Homer and Euripides. At the same time he was prepared to draw upon various Latin writers, including Plautus and Terence. Nevertheless what made Catullus so great was not his skill in reproducing or adapting earlier models, but the extraordinary originality and poignancy of the ideas which he was able to communicate through the inspired use of means bequeathed to him by other men—qualities given to no other Roman poet.

3 His Legacy to his Successors

While the poems of the other *noui poetae* hardly outlived their authors, those of Catullus exerted a powerful influence over his successors. Horace, who, as has been well said, 'followed the revolutionary idea of Catullus of adapting Greek lyric metres to Latin', borrows from him more than a dozen times in the *Odes*, and occasionally in the *Epodes*, *Satires*, and *Epistles*. Vergil is indebted to him again and again in the *Eclogues* and *Georgics*, and far more often in the *Aeneid*, his chief borrowings or echoes being from the *Peleus and Thetis*, which evidently made a great impression on him. Propertius and Tibullus drew freely on his writings, as did Ovid in every one of his numerous works. A century later Martial, more influenced than any other writer by Catullus and less weighed down by Roman *grauitas*, was to reflect his great predecessor on almost every page. The fame of Catullus lasted at least till the Second Century of our era, but, like the very different Lucretius, in the Dark Ages he was temporarily forgotten, and it was not till the Fourteenth Century that he emerged from the shadows. When a century or two later his poems at last became available in this country, they impressed a number of important writers and influenced their own compositions. Imitations, adaptations, and translations came from Skelton, Spenser, and Ben Jonson, followed by many other poets from Herrick to Byron, and verse translations and free paraphrases have come from numerous pens.

4 The Character of the Poems

The poems of Catullus cover a great range of subjects; they vary in length from two lines to over four hundred; and they differ widely in language, tone, and style. Some of them are in form conventional, though shot through with the poet's personality. Two only are translations, the one a close version of Callimachus, the other a free rendering of Sappho, so modified as to be virtually a new creation. The longest of the poems is a heroic narrative, told in the most dignified language and adorned with the learned allusions, figures of speech, and literary devices so dear to both Hellenistic and Roman readers. The same characteristics, combined with a tender naïveté, will be found in the two wedding-songs, the second of which is the most formal and symmetrical of all the poems. But however much Catullus might conform to an established literary pattern, he never disdained everyday words or simple turns of expression; he did not strain the resources of his native tongue in order to avoid calling a spade a spade; he did not, like Vergil, choose artificiality for its own sake and talk about odours bringing the wind, bees weaving granaries with flowers, or ships shaken out of their steersmen!

The great majority of the poems are concerned, not with legendary figures such as Ariadne, Berenice, or Attis, but with live persons known to the poet, loved and admired by him, or hated and despised. His feelings about them, and about himself, were clear and intense, and provided the material for poems which needed no ornaments or literary tricks or conformity with convention to make them memorable. In them he used not a 'poetic' vocabulary but the language of everyday, the plainest possible words, the simplest constructions, and at times the type of acceptable colloquial expression that adds spontaneity and freshness to so many of Cicero's letters and makes them so eminently readable. Using everyday language he was not afraid to admit a profusion of little words which the artificial poets of a later generation strove so hard to exclude. The simplicity of the language in some of the poems is quite extraordinary, for instance in his tribute to Cicero (no. 30), where there is not the least attempt at adornment of any kind. Moreover he not only chooses the simplest words: he puts every word in its natural place, making the writing of verse seem as easy as the writing of prose. Even in his more elaborate poems the same thing is noticeable; for instance in the description of his yacht and its voyage (no. 35), where in a most difficult metre the sentences flow with the utmost naturalness, and in the Attis (no. 65), where again metrical difficulties do not prevent him from writing *ego mulier, ego adulescens, ego ephebus, ego puer*—exactly the order which sense demands.

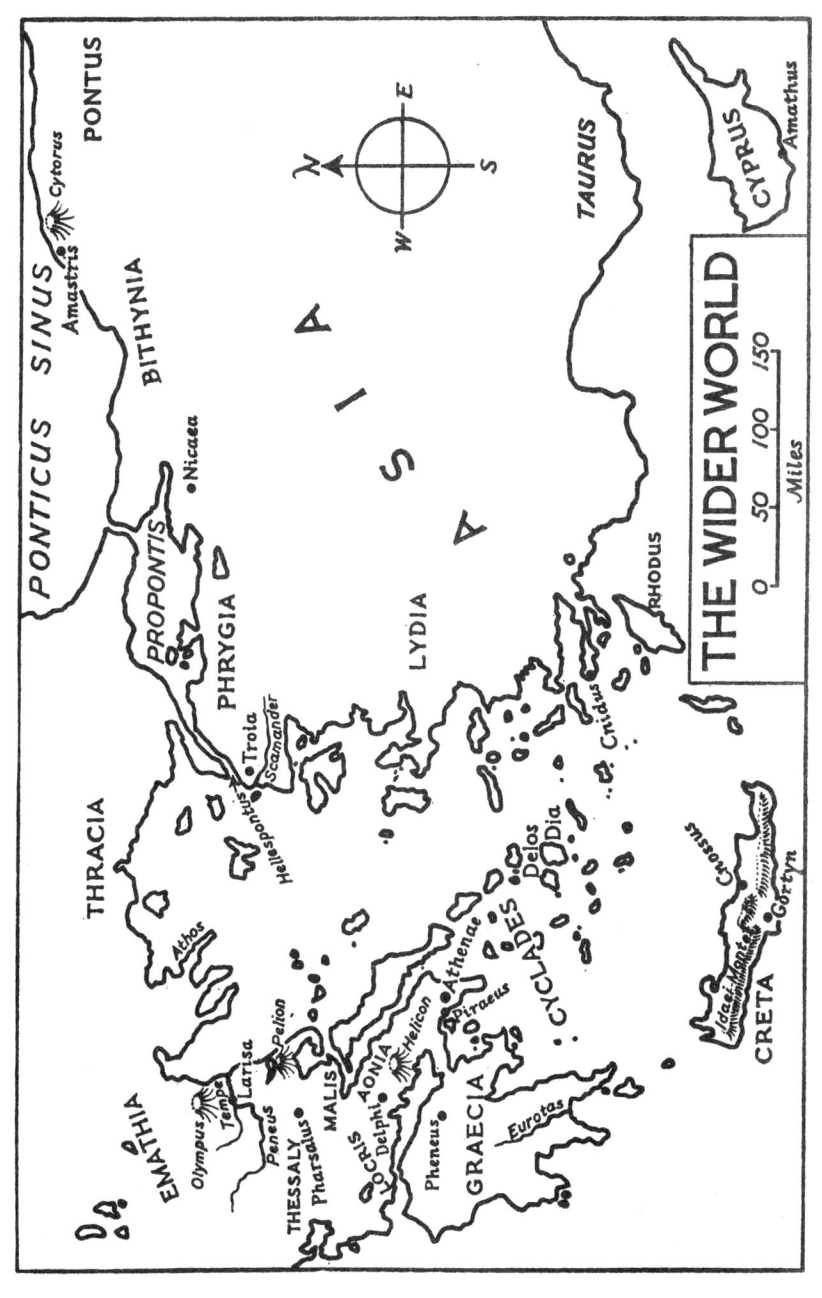

As stated above, the poems are chiefly concerned with live persons known to the poet. Those whom he loved he praised with the utmost warmth and affection; those who aroused his anger or scorn he denounced and abused with vehemence and derision, pulling no punches even when he assailed the mightiest in the land, including both 'great Caesar, the one and only general', and Pompey, known to the world as 'Great'. In not one poem is there the slightest trace of flattery. How different were the poets who followed him! Thirteen years after his death Vergil was hailing the twenty-two-year-old Octavian as a god to be worshipped with sacrifices; Horace went further and identified the then Augustus with Mercury, proclaiming him second to Jupiter himself; and Martial, the most Catullan of poets, grovelled obsequiously before the monster Domitian. However tempting the inducements of imperial patronage, however terrifying the threat of imperial wrath, we cannot believe that our most independent and free-speaking poet would ever have descended to this. About the living he indeed spoke freely: with the dead—save only those he had known and loved—he did not concern himself. Other poets sang the praises of Regulus, of the Scipios, of Marcellus; or like Juvenal they delivered scorching tirades against Tiberius and Domitian. Catullus did neither: apart from the phrases *Romuli nepotes* and *Romuli gens* there is no mention of any Roman of an earlier age, whether famous or infamous. He does not seem to have been interested in history; he was absorbed by his own experiences and by great literature, which inevitably meant Greek literature. He was not confined by the bonds of a narrow nationalistic outlook. And if he had little interest in the history of his nation, he had equally little in its geography, much as he adored Sirmio and Tibur. A glance at the first map, which shows every city, mountain, or river referred to in his poems, will reveal at once how few these references are. Not even Tiber is mentioned; not Italy itself. But in the second map it was impossible to show more than half the places which he names.

A word must be added about Catullus' versification. The metres—eleven in all—that are used in these poems are named in the Notes and explained in Appendix II. Comparison with the versification of later poets centres on the two most familiar of all Latin metres, Hexameters and Elegiacs. Those who are attuned to the ever-changing flow of Vergil's hexameters are likely to find Catullus' stiff and monotonous, lacking the 'true musical delight' which Milton found in English heroic verse; delight 'which consists only in apt numbers, fit quantity of syllables, and the sense variously drawn out from one verse into another'. But to those who can forget Vergil, Catullus' end-stopped lines —not unlike those which Shakespeare and Marlowe wrote at the same age—have a charm of their own, which is enhanced rather than diminished by the frequency of the dispondaic endings which later poets have led us to regard as peculiar. After all, there is a wealth of beautiful poetry that does not conform to the Miltonic rules. Has anything lovelier ever been written than the Psalms of David? How many of all the thousands of sentences that go to make up those hundred and fifty poems terminate anywhere but at the end of a line? But if it be granted that Catullan hexameters are stiff compared with those of later writers, in the case of Elegiacs it is the later writers who are stiff, and often excruciatingly monotonous, with their rigid limitation of the length of the sentence, which they force into the Procrustean bed of a single couplet, and the constant repetition of the same tricks of apposition, apostrophe, and padding which this rigidity necessitates. As for the other nine metres, above all the Hendecasyllabic, nothing could exceed the variety, grace, and effortless ease with which the poetry flows, often unaided by any of the recognised devices of the poet's craft.

5 The Verdict of Posterity

In Section 3 above attention was drawn to the borrowings which later poets have made from Catullus' writings. Apart from such borrowings we find many references to the poet, and many comments on his work. Propertius, who declared that Catullus had made Lesbia more famous than Helen herself, referred to him as *lasciuus*, an epithet applied to him by Ovid also. The word sometimes means 'lewd', but its usual meaning in Vergil, Horace, and Ovid is 'playful'. Observant readers will notice how often the words *ludo* and *ludus* appear in Catullus' poems. Tibullus, Ovid, and Martial all called him *doctus*, a description given to Lucretius also, but more often to Catullus than to any other poet; again Martial describes him as *tener*, an adjective of which the poet himself was very fond, and which admirably describes him. It was to reappear centuries later when Tennyson, who had such a lively appreciation of Catullus, Lucretius, and Vergil alike, referred to him not only as 'sweet Catullus' but as 'tenderest of Roman poets nineteen hundred years ago'. Other tributes by modern poets come from Macaulay, whom three of the poems (nos. 8, 54, and 55) always moved to tears, and from Swinburne, who addressed a poem to our author.

Prose writers have been equally enthusiastic. In the Seventeenth Century Fénelon set Catullus far above Ovid and Martial; in the last few decades he has been described by English scholars as 'the most passionate and brilliant, if not the greatest of Roman poets' (Palmer); as 'one of the most perfect of poets ... of infinitely higher lyrical genius than Horace' (Simpson); as 'a poet of exquisite pathos and tenderness, the equal of whom Rome was never again to see' (Melluish); and as 'the greatest lyrical poet of Rome' (Barber).

Such tributes should be respected but not taken on trust. Those who study the poems in this volume will not find it difficult to see why they have been and still are so greatly admired; but every reader, even the youngest, must form his own opinion.

Part One
SHORTER POEMS

you belong to me bitch!
o,yeah - sorry!

I FRIENDS AND FOES

(a) GOOD FRIENDS

1 CORNELIUS (i)

Dedication

CVI dono lepidum nouum libellum
arida modo pumice expolitum?
Corneli, tibi: namque tu solebas
meas esse aliquid putare nugas
iam tum, cum ausus es unus Italorum   5
omne aeuum tribus explicare chartis
doctis, Iuppiter, et laboriosis.
quare habe tibi quidquid hoc libelli
qualecumque; quod, [o] patrona uirgo,
plus uno maneat perenne saeclo.   10

I

2 CORNELIUS (ii)

A protestation of faithfulness

SI quicquam tacito commissum est fido ab amico,
  cuius sit penitus nota fides animi,
meque esse inuenies illorum iure sacratum,
  Corneli, et factum me esse puta Arpocratem.

CII

3 VERANIUS

A little poem that illustrates better than any other the warmth of Catullus' affection for the men he liked

VERANI, omnibus e meis amicis
antistans mihi milibus trecentis,
uenistine domum ad tuos penates

fratresque unanimos anumque matrem?
uenisti, o mihi nuntii beati! 5
uisam te incolumem audiamque Hiberum
narrantem loca, facta, nationes,
ut mos est tuus, applicansque collum
iucundum os oculosque suauiabor.
o quantum est hominum beatiorum, 10
quid me laetius est beatiusue?

IX

4 FABULLUS

A playful invitation, in which Catullus skilfully combines a warm tribute to his friend with a still warmer tribute to his mistress

CENABIS bene, mi Fabulle, apud me
paucis, si tibi di fauent, diebus,
si tecum attuleris bonam atque magnam
cenam, non sine candida puella
et uino et sale et omnibus cachinnis. 5
haec si, inquam, attuleris, uenuste noster,
cenabis bene; nam tui Catulli
plenus sacculus est araneurum.
sed contra accipies meros amores
seu quid suauius elegantiusue est: 10
nam unguentum dabo, quod meae puellae
donarunt Veneres Cupidinesque,
quod tu cum olfacies, deos rogabis,
totum ut te faciant, Fabulle, nasum.

XIII

5 VARUS

A playful colloquial poem, written after Catullus returned from Bithynia a year or two before his death

SHORTER POEMS   17

VARVS me meus ad suos amores
uisum duxerat e foro otiosum,
scortillum, ut mihi tum repente uisum est,
non sane illepidum neque inuenustum.
huc ut uenimus, incidere nobis   5
sermones uarii, in quibus, quid esset
iam Bithynia, quo modo se haberet,
et quonam mihi profuisset aere.
respondi id quod erat, nihil neque ipsis
nec praetoribus esse nec cohorti,   10
cur quisquam caput unctius referret,
praesertim quibus esset irrumator
praetor, nec faceret pili cohortem.
'at certe tamen,' inquiunt 'quod illic
natum dicitur esse, comparasti   15
ad lecticam homines.' ego, ut puellae
unum me facerem beatiorem,
'non' inquam 'mihi tam fuit maligne,
ut, prouincia quod mala incidisset,
non possem octo homines parare rectos.'   20
at mi nullus erat nec hic neque illic,
fractum qui ueteris pedem grabati
in collo sibi collocare posset.
hic illa, ut decuit cinaediorem,
'quaeso', inquit 'mihi, mi Catulle, paulum 25
istos commoda: nam uolo ad Serapim
deferri.' 'mane,' inquii puellae,
'istud quod modo dixeram me habere,
fugit me ratio: meus sodalis—
Cinna est Gaius,—is sibi parauit.   30
uerum, utrum illius an mei, quid ad me?
utor tam bene quam mihi pararim.
sed tu insulsa male et molesta uiuis,
per quam non licet esse neglegentem.'

                         X

6 Calvus (*i*)

Gentle fun at a friend's expense

RISI nescio quem modo e corona,
qui, cum mirifice Vatiniana
meus crimina Caluos explicasset,
admirans ait haec manusque tollens,
'di magni, salaputium disertum!' 5

LIII

7 Calvus (*ii*)

Sympathy with a friend in his bereavement

SI quicquam mutis gratum acceptumue sepulcris
  accidere a nostro, Calue, dolore potest,
quo desiderio ueteres renouamus amores
  atque olim missas flemus amicitias,
certe non tanto mors immatura dolori est 5
  Quintiliae, quantum gaudet amore tuo.

XCVI

(*b*) *DISAPPOINTING FRIENDS*

8 Cornificius

A cry for sympathy

MALEST, Cornifici, tuo Catullo,
malest me hercule, et laboriose,
et magis magis in dies et horas.
quem tu, quod minimum facillimumque est,
qua solatus es allocutione?
irascor tibi. sic meos amores?
paulum quid lubet allocutionis, 5
maestius lacrimis Simonideis.

XXXVIII

9 Gellius (i)

A bitter reproach

NON ideo, Gelli, sperabam te mihi fidum
    in misero hoc nostro, hoc perdito amore fore,
quod te cognossem bene constantemue putarem
    aut posse a turpi mentem inhibere probro;
et quamuis tecum multo coniungerer usu,   5
    non satis id causae credideram esse tibi.
tu satis id duxti: tantum tibi gaudium in omni
    culpa est, in quacumque est aliquid sceleris.

XCI

10 Gellius (ii)

A warning of vengeance to come

SAEPE tibi studioso animo uenante requirens
    carmina uti possem mittere Battiadae,
qui te lenirem nobis, neu conarere
    tela infesta [meum] mittere in usque caput,
hunc uideo mihi nunc frustra sumptum esse laborem,   5
    Gelli, nec nostras hic ualuisse preces.
contra nos tela ista tua euitabimus †amitha
    at fixus nostris tu dabis supplicium.

CXVI

11 An Unnamed Friend

A sad lament over broken faith

DESINE de quoquam quicquam bene uelle mereri
    aut aliquem fieri posse putare pium.
omnia sunt ingrata, nihil fecisse benigne
    [prodest,] immo etiam taedet obestque magis;
ut mihi, quem nemo grauius nec acerbius urget   5
    quam modo qui me unum atque unicum amicum habuit.

LXXIII

12 Alfenus

A longer plaint on the same theme

ALFENE immemor atque unanimis false sodalibus,
iam te nil miseret, dure, tui dulcis amiculi?
iam me prodere, iam non dubitas fallere, perfide?
nec facta impia fallacum hominum caelicolis placent.
quae tu neglegis ac me miserum deseris in malis. 5
eheu quid faciant, dic, homines cuiue habeant fidem?
certe tute iubebas animam tradere, inique, [me]
inducens in amorem, quasi tuta omnia mi forent.
idem nunc retrahis te ac tua dicta omnia factaque
uentos irrita ferre ac nebulas aerias sinis. 10
si tu oblitus es, at di meminerunt, meminit Fides,
quae te ut paeniteat postmodo facti faciet tui.

XXX

(c) FOES

13 Ravidus

A threat to a rival

QUAENAM te mala mens, miselle Rauide,
agit praecipitem in meos iambos?
quis deus tibi non bene aduocatus
uecordem parat excitare rixam?
an ut peruenias in ora uulgi? 5
quid uis? qualubet esse notus optas?
eris, quandoquidem meos amores
cum longa uoluisti amare poena.

XL

14 Caesar (i)

A snub for the great man

NIL nimium studeo, Caesar, tibi uelle placere,
nec scire utrum sis albus an ater homo.

XCIII

SHORTER POEMS

15 CAESAR (ii)

A warning of more to come

IRASCERE iterum meis iambis
inmerentibus, unice imperator.

LIV B

(d) FRIENDS AND FOES CONTRASTED

16 PORCIUS AND SOCRATION: FABULLUS AND VERANIUS

A protest at the prosperity of the wicked

PORCI et Socration, duae sinistrae
Pisonis, scabies famesque mundi,
uos Veraniolo meo et Fabullo
uerpus praeposuit Priapus ille?
uos conuiuia lauta sumptuose   5
de die facitis, mei sodales
quaerunt in triuio uocationes?

XLVII

17 MARRUCINUS: POLLIO, FABULLUS, AND VERANIUS

A denunciation of a petty thief

MARRUCINE Asini, manu sinistra
non belle uteris: in ioco atque uino
tollis lintea neglegentiorum.
hoc salsum esse putas? fugit te, inepte:
quamuis sordida res et inuenusta est.   5
non credis mihi? crede Pollioni
fratri, qui tua furta uel talento
mutari uelit: est enim leporum
differtus puer et facetiarum.
quare aut hendecasyllabos trecentos   10
exspecta, aut mihi linteum remitte,
quod me non mouet aestimatione,

uerum est mnemosynum mei sodalis.
nam sudaria Saetaba ex Hiberis
miserunt mihi muneri Fabullus   15
et Veranius: haec amem necesse est
ut Veraniolum meum et Fabullum.

XII

(e) OBJECTIONABLE PEOPLE

18 EGNATIUS

An exposure of a rival's nasty habits

EGNATIUS, quod candidos habet dentes,
renidet usque quaque. si ad rei uentum est
subsellium, cum orator excitat fletum,
renidet ille; si ad pii rogum fili
lugetur, orba cum flet unicum mater,   5
renidet ille. quidquid est, ubicumque est,
quodcumque agit, renidet: hunc habet morbum,
neque elegantem, ut arbitror, neque urbanum.
quare monendum est [te] mihi, bone Egnati.
si urbanus esses aut Sabinus aut Tiburs   10
aut pinguis Vmber aut obesus Etruscus
aut Lanuuinus ater atque dentatus
aut Transpadanus, ut meos quoque attingam,
aut quilubet, qui puriter lauit dentes,
tamen renidere usque quaque te nollem: 15
nam risu inepto res ineptior nulla est.
nunc Celtiber [es]: Celtiberia in terra,
quod quisque minxit, hoc sibi solet mane
dentem atque russam defricare gingiuam,
ut, quo iste uester expolitior dens est,   20
hoc te amplius bibisse praedicet loti.

XXXIX

SHORTER POEMS

19 ARRIUS

Scorn for a silly affectation

CHOMMODA dicebat, si quando commoda uellet
   dicere, et insidias Arrius hinsidias,
et tum mirifice sperabat se esse locutum,
   cum quantum poterat dixerat hinsidias.
credo, sic mater, sic liber auunculus eius,   5
   sic maternus auus dixerat atque auia.
hoc misso in Syriam requierant omnibus aures:
   audibant eadem haec leniter et leuiter,
nec sibi postilla metuebant talia uerba,
   cum subito affertur nuntius horribilis,   10
Ionios fluctus, postquam illuc Arrius isset,
   iam non Ionios esse sed Hionios.

                               LXXXIV

20 COMINIUS

Judgment on a very nasty old man

SI, Comini, populi arbitrio tua cana senectus
   spurcata impuris moribus intereat,
non equidem dubito quin primum inimica bonorum
   lingua exsecta auido sit data uulturio,
effossos oculos uoret atro gutture coruus,
   intestina canes, cetera membra lupi.

                               CVIII

21 MAMURRA (i)

Condemnation of a spendthrift

FIRMANO saltu non falso Mentula diues
   fertur, qui tot res in se habet egregias,
aucupium omne genus, piscis, prata, arua ferasque.
   nequiquam: fructus sumptibus exsuperat.
quare concedo sit diues, dum omnia desint.   5
   saltum laudemus, dum †modo ipse egeat.

                               CXIV

II POETS AND ORATORS

(a) GOOD

22 CAECILIUS

A tribute to a promising poet

POETAE tenero, meo sodali,
uelim Caecilio, papyre, dicas
Veronam ueniat, Noui relinquens
Comi moenia Lariumque litus.
nam quasdam uolo cogitationes   5
amici accipiat sui meique.
quare, si sapiet, uiam uorabit,
quamuis candida milies puella
euntem reuocet, manusque collo
ambas iniciens roget morari.   10
quae nunc, si mihi uera nuntiantur,
illum deperit impotente amore.
nam quo tempore legit incohatam
Dindymi dominam, ex eo misellae
ignes interiorem edunt medullam.   15
ignosco tibi, Sapphica puella
musa doctior; est enim uenuste
Magna Caecilio incohata Mater.

XXXV

23 CALVUS (*iii*)

A good-humoured warning to a rival poet

HESTERNO, Licini, die otiosi
multum lusimus in meis tabellis,
ut conuenerat esse delicatos:
scribens uersiculos uterque nostrum

ludebat numero modo hoc modo illoc, 5
reddens mutua per iocum atque uinum.
atque illinc abii tuo lepore
incensus, Licini, facetiisque,
ut nec me miserum cibus iuuaret
nec somnus tegeret quiete ocellos, 10
sed toto indomitus furore lecto
uersarer, cupiens uidere lucem,
ut tecum loquerer simulque ut essem.
at defessa labore membra postquam
semimortua lectulo iacebant, 15
hoc, iucunde, tibi poema feci,
ex quo perspiceres meum dolorem.
nunc audax caue sis, precesque nostras,
oramus, caue despuas, ocelle,
ne poenas Nemesis reposcat a te. 20
est uemens dea: laedere hanc caueto.
        L

(*b*) *BAD*

24 SUFFENUS

A restrained rebuke for a too prolific poet

SUFFENUS iste, Vare, quem probe nosti,
homo est uenustus et dicax et urbanus,
idemque longe plurimos facit uersus.
puto esse ego illi milia aut decem aut plura
perscripta, nec sic ut fit in palimpseston 5
relata: cartae regiae, noui libri,
noui umbilici, lora rubra membranae,
derecta plumbo et pumice omnia aequata.
haec cum legas tu, bellus ille et urbanus
Suffenus unus caprimulgus aut fossor 10
rursus uidetur: tantum abhorret ac mutat.
hoc quid putemus esse? qui modo scurra
aut si quid hac re scitius uidebatur,

idem infaceto est infacetior rure,
simul poemata attigit, neque idem umquam   15
aeque est beatus ac poema cum scribit:
tam gaudet in se tamque se ipse miratur.
nimirum idem omnes fallimur, neque est quisquam
quem non in aliqua re uidere Suffenum
possis. suus cuique attributus est error;   20
sed non uidemus manticae quod in tergo est.

XXII

25 Suffenus, Caesius, and Aquinus

A threat of retaliation for a practical joke

NI te plus oculis meis amarem,
iucundissime Calue, munere isto
odissem te odio Vatiniano:
nam quid feci ego quidue sum locutus,
cur me tot male perderes poetis?   5
isti di mala multa dent clienti,
qui tantum tibi misit impiorum.
quod si, ut suspicor, hoc nouum ac repertum
munus dat tibi Sulla litterator,
non est mi male, sed bene ac beate,   10
quod non dispereunt tui labores.
di magni, horribilem et sacrum libellum!
quem tu scilicet ad tuum Catullum
misti, continuo ut die periret,
Saturnalibus, optimo dierum!   15
non non hoc tibi, false, sic abibit.
nam, si luxerit, ad librariorum
curram scrinia, Caesios, Aquinos,
Suffenum, omnia colligam uenena,
ac te his suppliciis remunerabor.   20
uos hinc interea ualete abite
illuc, unde malum pedem attulistis,
saecli incommoda, pessimi poetae.

XIV

26 Sestius

A confession of greed deservedly punished

O FVNDE noster seu Sabine seu Tiburs
(nam te esse Tiburtem autumant, quibus non est
cordi Catullum laedere; at quibus cordi est,
quouis Sabinum pignore esse contendunt),
sed seu Sabine siue uerius Tiburs, 5
fui libenter in tua suburbana
uilla, malamque pectore expuli tussim,
non inmerenti quam mihi meus uenter,
dum sumptuosas appeto, dedit, cenas.
nam, Sestianus dum uolo esse conuiua, 10
orationem in Antium petitorem
plenam ueneni et pestilentiae legi.
hic me grauedo frigida et frequens tussis
quassauit usque, dum in tuum sinum fugi,
et me recuraui otioque et urtica. 15
quare refectus maximas tibi grates
ago, meum quod non es ulta peccatum.
nec deprecor iam, si nefaria scripta
Sesti recepso, quin grauedinem et tussim
non mi, sed ipsi Sestio ferat frigus, 20
qui tunc uocat me, cum malum librum legi.

XLIV

27 Volusius

A very rude onslaught on a wretched scribbler

ANNALES Volusi, cacata carta,
uotum soluite pro mea puella.
nam sanctae Veneri Cupidinique
uouit, si sibi restitutus essem
desissemque truces uibrare iambos, 5
electissima pessimi poetae
scripta tardipedi deo daturam

infelicibus ustulanda lignis.
et hoc pessima se puella uidit
iocose lepide uouere diuis.   10
nunc o caeruleo creata ponto,
quae sanctum Idalium Vriosque apertos
quaeque Ancona Cnidumque harundinosam
colis quaeque Amathunta quaeque Golgos
quaeque Durrachium Hadriae tabernam,   15
acceptum face redditumque uotum,
si non illepidum neque inuenustum est.
at uos interea uenite in ignem,
pleni ruris et inficetiarum
annales Volusi, cacata carta.   20
         XXXVI

28 Mamurra (*ii*)

What a bad poet must expect

MENTULA conatur Pipleium scandere montem:
Musae furcillis praecipitem eiciunt.
         CV

(c) GOOD AND BAD CONTRASTED

29 Cinna: Hortensius and Volusius

A warning that a long poem may have a short life

ZMYRNA mei Cinnae nonam post denique messem
 quam coepta est nonamque edita post hiemem,
milia cum interea quingenta Hortensius uno
  . . . . .
Zmyrna cauas Satrachi penitus mittetur ad undas, 5
 Zmyrnam cana diu saecula peruoluent.
at Volusi annales Paduam morientur ad ipsam
 et laxas scombris saepe dabunt tunicas.
         XCV

30 Cicero: Catullus

A tribute to a great advocate

DISERTISSIME Romuli nepotum,
quot sunt quotque fuere, Marce Tulli,
quotque post aliis erunt in annis,
gratias tibi maximas Catullus
agit pessimus omnium poeta, 5
tanto pessimus omnium poeta,
quanto tu optimus omnium patronus.

XLIX

III THE LOST BROTHER

31 FUNERAL OFFERINGS

A poignant lament at the grave of one dearly loved

MVLTAS per gentes et multa per aequora uectus
   aduenio has miseras, frater, ad inferias,
ut te postremo donarem munere mortis
   et mutam nequiquam alloquerer cinerem.
quandoquidem fortuna mihi tete abstulit ipsum,   5
   heu miser indigne frater adempte mihi,
nunc tamen interea haec, prisco quae more parentum
   tradita sunt tristi munere ad inferias,
accipe fraterno multum manantia fletu,
   atque in perpetuum, frater, aue atque uale.   10

32 TOO SAD TO WRITE (*i*)

An apology for a promise unfulfilled

ETSI me assiduo confectus cura dolore
   seuocat a doctis, Ortale, uirginibus,
nec potis est dulcis Musarum expromere fetus
   mens animi, tantis fluctuat ipsa malis—
namque mei nuper Lethaeo gurgite fratris   5
   pallidulum manans alluit unda pedem,
Troia Rhoeteo quem subter litore tellus
   ereptum nostris obterit ex oculis.

    .   .   .   .   .   .

   numquam ego te, uita frater amabilior,   10
aspiciam posthac? at certe semper amabo,
   semper maesta tua carmina morte canam,
qualia sub densis ramorum concinit umbris

Daulias, absumpti fata gemens Ityli.—
 sed tamen in tantis maeroribus, Ortale, mitto 15
  haec expressa tibi carmina Battiadae,
ne tua dicta uagis nequiquam credita uentis
  effluxisse meo forte putes animo,
ut missum sponsi furtiuo munere malum
  procurrit casto uirginis e gremio, 20
quod miserae oblitae molli sub ueste locatum,
  dum aduentu matris prosilit, excutitur,
atque illud prono praeceps agitur decursu,
  huic manat tristi conscius ore rubor.

            LXV

Poem's strength lies in balance between Catullus' sadness at the inadequacy of the ceremony he has come to perform and the confident assumption that the understanding between him and his brother will overcome this inadequacy.

IV HOME

33 BACK FROM PHRYGIA

The poet's rapture at the thought of his journey home

IAM uer egelidos refert tepores,
iam caeli furor aequinoctialis
iucundis Zephyri silescit aureis.
linquantur Phrygii, Catulle, campi
Nicaeaeque ager uber aestuosae: 5
ad claras Asiae uolemus urbes.
iam mens praetrepidans auet uagari,
iam laeti studio pedes uigescunt.
o dulces comitum ualete coetus,
longe quos simul a domo profectos 10
diuersae uarie uiae reportant.

XLVI

34 SIRMIO

A captivating description of the place the poet loved above all others

PAENE insularum, Sirmio, insularumque
ocelle, quascumque in liquentibus stagnis
marique uasto fert uterque Neptunus,
quam te libenter quamque laetus inuiso,
uix mi ipse credens Thuniam atque Bithunos 5
liquisse campos et uidere te in tuto.
o quid solutis est beatius curis,
cum mens onus reponit, ac peregrino
labore fessi uenimus larem ad nostrum,
desideratoque acquiescimus lecto? 10
hoc est quod unum est pro laboribus tantis.

SHORTER POEMS

salue, o uenusta Sirmio, atque ero gaude
gaudente, uosque, o Lydiae lacus undae,
ridete quidquid est domi cachinnorum.

XXXI

35 THE PINNACE

The life-story of a faithful friend

PHASELVS ille, quem uidetis, hospites,
ait fuisse nauium celerrimus,
neque ullius natantis impetum trabis
nequisse praeterire, siue palmulis
opus foret uolare siue linteo. 5
et hoc negat minacis Hadriatici
negare litus insulasue Cycladas
Rhodumque nobilem horridamque Thraciam
Propontida trucemue Ponticum sinum,
ubi iste post phaselus antea fuit 10
comata silua; nam Cytorio in iugo
loquente saepe sibilum edidit coma.
Amastri Pontica et Cytore buxifer,
tibi haec fuisse et esse cognitissima
ait phaselus: ultima ex origine 15
tuo stetisse dicit in cacumine,
tuo imbuisse palmulas in aequore,
et inde tot per impotentia freta
erum tulisse, laeua siue dextera
uocaret aura, siue utrumque Iuppiter 20
simul secundus incidisset in pedem;
neque ulla uota litoralibus deis
sibi esse facta, cum ueniret a mari
nouissimo hunc ad usque limpidum lacum.
sed haec prius fuere: nunc recondita 25
senet quiete seque dedicat tibi,
gemelle Castor et gemelle Castoris.

IV

V. LESBIA

(a) HAPPY DAYS

36 THE ENRAPTURED LOVER

A masterly translation of a superb lyric

ILLE mi par esse deo uidetur,
ille, si fas est, superare diuos,
qui sedens aduersus identidem te
    spectat et audit
dulce ridentem, misero quod omnis   **5**
eripit sensus mihi: nam simul te,
Lesbia, aspexi, nihil est super mi
     . . . . .
lingua sed torpet, tenuis sub artus
flamma demanat, sonitu suopte
tintinnant aures, gemina teguntur   **10**
    lumina nocte.

LI 1-12

37 KISSES FOR YOU

The lure of present joys

VIVAMUS, mea Lesbia, atque amemus,
rumoresque senum seueriorum
omnes unius aestimemus assis!
soles occidere et redire possunt:
nobis cum semel occidit breuis lux,
nox est perpetua una dormienda.
da mi basia mille, deinde centum,
dein mille altera, dein secunda centum,
deinde usque altera milia, deinde centum.

34

SHORTER POEMS

    dein, cum milia multa fecerimus,   10
    conturbabimus illa, ne sciamus,
    aut ne quis malus inuidere possit,
    cum tantum sciat esse basiorum.

                                  V

38 KISSES FOR ME

Passion without limit

    QVAERIS, quot mihi basiationes
    tuae, Lesbia, sint satis superque.
    quam magnus numerus Libyssae harenae
    lasarpiciferis iacet Cyrenis
    oraclum Iouis inter aestuosi   5
    et Batti ueteris sacrum sepulcrum;
    aut quam sidera multa, cum tacet nox,
    furtiuos hominum uident amores:
    tam te basia multa basiare
    uesano satis et super Catullo est,   10
    quae nec pernumerare curiosi
    possint nec mala fascinare lingua.

                                  VII

39 QUINTIA? No!

Excellent parts, but not a perfect whole

    QVINTIA formosa est multis. mihi candida, longa,
      recta est: haec ego sic singula confiteor.
    totum illud formosa nego: nam nulla uenustas,
      nulla in tam magno est corpore mica salis.
    Lesbia formosa est, quae cum pulcerrima tota est,   5
      tum omnibus una omnis surripuit Veneres.

                                LXXXVI

40 Mamurra's Mistress? No!

An odious comparison repudiated

SALVE, nec minimo puella naso
nec bello pede nec nigris ocellis
nec longis digitis nec ore sicco
nec sane nimis elegante lingua,
decoctoris amica Formiani.　　　　　　　　5
ten prouincia narrat esse bellam?
tecum Lesbia nostra comparatur?
o saeclum insapiens at infacetum!

XLIII

41 The Sparrow (i)

High praise for a little bird

PASSER, deliciae meae puellae,
quicum ludere, quem in sinu tenere,
cui primum digitum dare appetenti
et acris solet incitare morsus,
cum desiderio meo nitenti　　　　　　　　5
carum nescio quid lubet iocari,
et solaciolum sui doloris,
credo, ut tum grauis acquiescat ardor:
tecum ludere sicut ipsa possem
et tristis animi leuare curas!

II 1–10

42 The Sparrow (ii)

A tender, but not too serious, lament

LVGETE, o Veneres Cupidinesque,
et quantum est hominum uenustiorum:
passer mortuus est meae puellae,
passer, deliciae meae puellae,
quem plus illa oculis suis amabat.　　　　　5
nam mellitus erat suamque norat

ipsam tam bene quam puella matrem,
nec sese a gremio illius mouebat,
sed circumsiliens modo huc modo illuc
ad solam dominam usque pipiabat;   10
qui nunc it per iter tenebricosum
illud, unde negant redire quemquam.
at uobis male sit, malae tenebrae
Orci, quae omnia bella deuoratis:
tam bellum mihi passerem abstulistis.   15
o factum male! o miselle passer!
tua nunc opera meae puellae
flendo turgiduli rubent ocelli.

III

(b) DOUBT

43 THE PROMISED FRIENDSHIP

An unsure hope that Lesbia will keep her word

IVCVNDVM, mea uita, mihi proponis amorem
    hunc nostrum inter nos perpetuumque fore.
di magni, facite ut uere promittere possit,
    atque id sincere dicat et ex animo,
ut liceat nobis tota perducere uita
    aeternum hoc sanctae foedus amicitiae.

CIX

44 PROMISES MADE TO BE BROKEN

The fading of hope

NVLLI se dicit mulier mea nubere malle
    quam mihi, non si se Iuppiter ipse petat.
dicit: sed mulier cupido quod dicit amanti,
    in uento et rapida scribere oportet aqua.

LXX

POEMS OF CATULLUS

45 LESBIA'S TONGUE
The last glimmer of hope

LESBIA mi dicit semper male nec tacet umquam
de me: Lesbia me dispeream nisi amat.
quo signo? quia sunt totidem mea: deprecor illam
assidue, uerum dispeream nisi amo.

XCII

46 I KNOW HER NOW
A declaration of distaste for the loved one

DICEBAS quondam solum te nosse Catullum,
Lesbia, nec prae me uelle tenere Iouem.
dilexi tum te non tantum ut uulgus amicam,
sed pater ut gnatos diligit et generos.
nunc te cognoui: quare etsi impensius uror,
multo mi tamen es uilior et leuior.
qui potis est, inquis? quod amantem iniuria talis
cogit amare magis, sed bene uelle minus.

LXXII

47 NONE WAS EVER LOVED SO DEARLY
All the blame laid on Lesbia

NVLLA potest mulier tantum se dicere amatam
uere, quantum a me Lesbia amata mea est.
nulla fides ullo fuit umquam foedere tanta,
quanta in amore tuo ex parte reperta mea est.

LXXXVII

48 I LOVE HER STILL
A declaration that love survives distaste

HVC est mens deducta tua mea, Lesbia, culpa
atque ita se officio perdidit ipsa suo,
ut iam nec bene uelle tibi, si optima fias,
nec desistere amare, omnia si facias.

LXXV

SHORTER POEMS

(c) THE BREAK

49 My Friend has Robbed me of My Love

Grief at the worst of all breaches of faith

RVFE mihi frustra ac nequiquam credite amice
   (frustra? immo magno cum pretio atque malo),
sicine subrepsti mi, atque intestina perurens
   ei misero eripuisti omnia nostra bona?
eripuisti, heu heu nostrae crudele uenenum
   uitae, heu heu nostrae pestis amicitiae.

LXXVII

50 Is Reconciliation possible?

Hope revived for a moment

SI quicquam cupido optantique optigit umquam
   insperanti, hoc est gratum animo proprie.
quare hoc est gratum †nobis quoque† carius auro
   quod te restituis, Lesbia, mi cupido.
restituis cupido atque insperanti, ipsa refers te
   nobis. o lucem candidiore nota!
quis me uno uiuit felicior, aut magis †hac est
   †optandus uita dicere quis poterit?

CVII

51 Never again!

A heart-broken confession that hope and love are dead

FVRI et Aureli, comites Catulli,
siue in extremos penetrabit Indos,
litus ut longe resonante Eoa
   tunditur unda,
siue in Hyrcanos Arabasue molles,
seu Sagas sagittiferosue Parthos,
siue quae septemgeminus colorat
   aequora Nilus,

40 POEMS OF CATULLUS

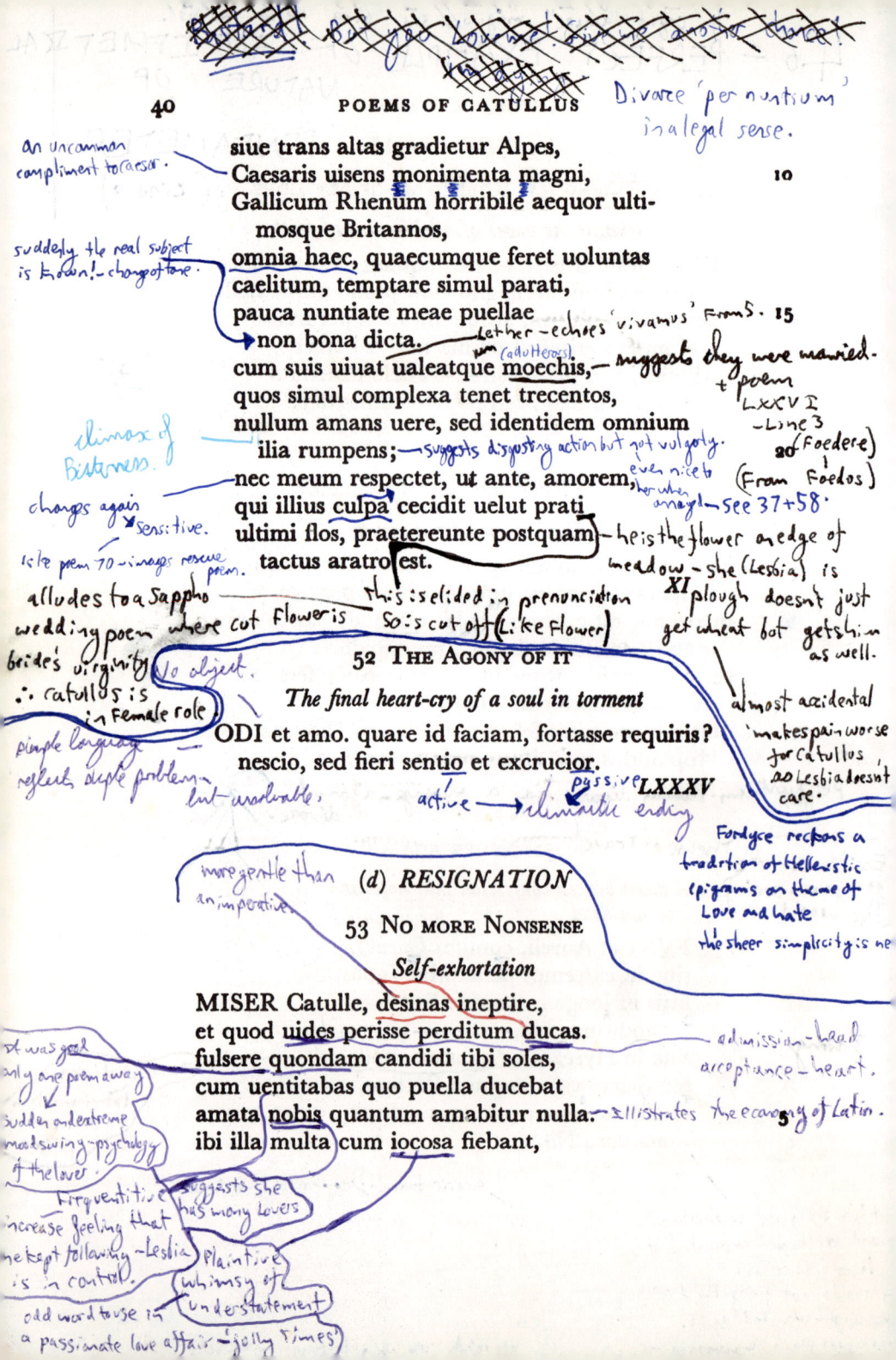

siue trans altas gradietur Alpes,
Caesaris uisens monimenta magni,
Gallicum Rhenum horribile aequor ulti-
    mosque Britannos,
omnia haec, quaecumque feret uoluntas
caelitum, temptare simul parati,
pauca nuntiate meae puellae
non bona dicta.
cum suis uiuat ualeatque moechis,
quos simul complexa tenet trecentos,
nullum amans uere, sed identidem omnium
    ilia rumpens;
nec meum respectet, ut ante, amorem,
qui illius culpa cecidit uelut prati
ultimi flos, praetereunte postquam
    tactus aratro est.

52 THE AGONY OF IT

The final heart-cry of a soul in torment

ODI et amo. quare id faciam, fortasse requiris?
nescio, sed fieri sentio et excrucior.

LXXXV

(d) RESIGNATION

53 NO MORE NONSENSE

Self-exhortation

MISER Catulle, desinas ineptire,
et quod uides perisse perditum ducas.
fulsere quondam candidi tibi soles,
cum uentitabas quo puella ducebat
amata nobis quantum amabitur nulla.
ibi illa multa cum iocosa fiebant,

SHORTER POEMS 41

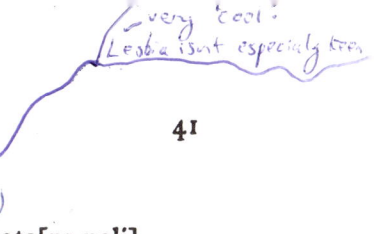

quae tu uolebas nec puella nolebat.
fulsere uere candidi tibi soles.
nunc iam illa non uolt: tu quoque inpote[ns noli],
nec quae fugit sectare, nec miser uiue, 10
sed obstinata mente perfer, obdura.
uale, puella. iam Catullus obdurat,
nec te requiret nec rogabit inuitam.
at tu dolebis, cum rogaberis nulla.
scelesta, uae te, quae tibi manet uita? 15
quis nunc te adibit? cui uideberis bella?
quem nunc amabis? cuius esse diceris?
quem basiabis? cui labella mordebis?
at tu, Catulle, destinatus obdura.

VIII

54 OH TO FORGET!

A plea for deliverance from mental sickness

SIQVA recordanti benefacta priora uoluptas
  est homini, cum se cogitat esse pium,
nec sanctam uiolasse fidem, nec foedere nullo
  diuum ad fallendos numine abusum homines,
multa parata manent in longa aetate, Catulle, 5
  ex hoc ingrato gaudia amore tibi.
nam quaecumque homines bene cuiquam aut dicere possunt
  aut facere, haec a te dictaque factaque sunt.
omnia quae ingratae perierunt credita menti.
  quare iam te cur amplius excrucies? 10
quin tu animo offirmas atque istinc teque reducis,
  et dis inuitis desinis esse miser?
difficile est longum subito deponere amorem.
  difficile est, uerum hoc qua lubet efficias:
una salus haec est, hoc est tibi peruincendum, 15
  hoc facias, siue id non pote siue pote.
o di, si uestrum est misereri, aut si quibus umquam
  extremam iam ipsa in morte tulistis opem,

me miserum aspicite et, si uitam puriter egi,
   eripite hanc pestem perniciemque mihi, 20
quae mihi subrepens imos ut torpor in artus
   expulit ex omni pectore laetitias.
non iam illud quaero, contra me ut diligat illa,
   aut, quod non potis est, esse pudica uelit:
ipse ualere opto et taetrum hunc deponere morbum. 25
   o di, reddite mi hoc pro pietate mea.
LXXVI

VI VARIED THEMES

55 THE MORTGAGE

A wry pun

FVRI, uillula uestra non ad Austri
flatus opposita est neque ad Fauoni
nec saeui Boreae aut Apheliotae,
uerum ad milia quindecim et ducentos.
o uentum horribilem atque pestilentem!   5
                      XXVI

56 NO WATER, PLEASE!

A call for strong drink

MINISTER uetuli puer Falerni
inger mi calices amariores,
ut lex Postumiae iubet magistrae
ebrioso acino ebriosioris.
at uos quo lubet hinc abite, lymphae,   5
uini pernicies, et ad seueros
migrate. hic merus est Thyonianus.
                      XXVII

57 THE HARD-HEARTED ONE

A cliché *newly applied*

NVM te leaena montibus Libystinis
aut Scylla latrans infima inguinum parte
tam mente dura procreauit ac taetra,
ut supplicis uocem in nouissimo casu
contemptam haberes, a nimis fero corde?   5
                      LX

44 POEMS OF CATULLUS

58 SWEET LOVERS

A eulogy of young love

ACMEN Septimius suos amores
tenens in gremio 'mea' inquit 'Acme,
ni te perdite amo atque amare porro
omnes sum assiduo paratus annos,
quantum qui pote plurimum perire, 5
solus in Libya Indiaque tosta
caesio ueniam obuius leoni.'
hoc ut dixit, Amor sinistra ut ante
dextra sternuit approbationem.

    at Acme leuiter caput reflectens 10
et dulcis pueri ebrios ocellos
illo purpureo ore suauiata,
'sic', inquit 'mea uita Septimille,
huic uni domino usque seruiamus,
ut multo mihi maior acriorque 15
ignis mollibus ardet in medullis.'
hoc ut dixit, Amor sinistra ut ante
dextra sternuit approbationem.

    nunc ab auspicio bono profecti
mutuis animis amant amantur. 20
unam Septimius misellus Acmen
mauult quam Syrias Britanniasque:
uno in Septimio fidelis Acme
facit delicias libidinesque.
quis ullos homines beatiores 25
uidit, quis Venerem auspicatiorem?

XLV
59 THROW HIM FROM THE BRIDGE!

A jest at the expense of a neighbour, and of a neighbouring town

O COLONIA, quae cupis ponte ludere longo,
et salire paratum habes, sed uereris inepta

SHORTER POEMS 45

```
crura ponticuli axulis stantis in rediuiuis,
ne supinus eat cauaque in palude recumbat:
sic tibi bonus ex tua pons libidine fiat,                    5
in quo uel Salisubsali sacra suscipiantur,
munus hoc mihi maximi da, Colonia, risus.
quendam municipem meum de tuo uolo ponte
ire praecipitem in lutum per caputque pedesque,
uerum totius ut lacus putidaeque paludis                     10
liuidissima maximeque est profunda uorago.
insulsissimus est homo, nec sapit pueri instar
bimuli tremula patris dormientis in ulna.
cui cum sit uiridissimo nupta flore puella
et puella tenellulo delicatior haedo,                        15
adseruanda nigerrimis diligentius uuis,
ludere hanc sinit ut lubet, nec pili facit uni,
nec se subleuat ex sua parte, sed uelut alnus
in fossa Liguri iacet suppernata securi,
tantundem omnia sentiens quam si nulla sit umquam:           20
talis iste meus stupor nil uidet, nihil audit,
ipse qui sit, utrum sit an non sit, id quoque nescit.
nunc eum uolo de tuo ponte mittere pronum,
si pote stolidum repente excitare ueternum,
et supinum animum in graui derelinquere caeno,               25
ferream ut soleam tenaci in uoragine mula.
```

XVII

60 HYMN TO DIANA

The praises of a many-sided deity

DIANAE sumus in fide
puellae et pueri integri:
[Dianam pueri integri]
   puellaeque canamus.
o Latonia, maximi   5
magna progenies Iouis,

46 POEMS OF CATULLUS

> quam mater prope Deliam
>   deposiuit oliuam,
> montium domina ut fores
> siluarumque uirentium   10
> saltuumque reconditorum
>   amniumque sonantum;
> tu Lucina dolentibus
> Iuno dicta puerperis,
> tu potens Triuia et notho es   15
>   dicta lumine Luna.
> tu cursu, dea, menstruo
> metiens iter annuum,
> rustica agricolae bonis
>   tecta frugibus exples.   20
> sis quocumque tibi placet
> sancta nomine, Romulique,
> antique ut solita es, bona
>   sospites ope gentem.
>
>   XXXIV

Margin annotations:
- Archaism old/solemn. (→ deposiuit oliuam)
- so that you might be (→ ut fores)
- conventional in hymns. — Anaphora — repetition of words
- originally epithet of Hecate. (→ Triuia)
- Because Diana had some associations with childbirth, she became associated with Juno who presided over it.
- They got confused because the distinction was not totally clear. i.e. when Diana was doing same job as another goddess, she took on the same name.
- Catullus is hedging his bets — calling Diana in as many ways as poss.
- Be thou Hallowed (→ sis ... sancta nomine)
- Solemn Hymn Language (safe)

Greek Hymn.
     Conventional structure.

① Introduction
② Invocation of Goddess + details of ancestry.
③ Spheres of concern.
④ One of those spheres is related to petitioners.
⑤ prayer that goddess will continue to help.

Part Two

LONGER POEMS

61 TOO SAD TO WRITE (*ii*)

An apology for inability to fulfil a friend's request
The poet is too distressed to write frivolous verse

QVOD mihi fortuna casuque oppressus acerbo
   conscriptum hoc lacrimis mittis epistolium,
naufragum ut eiectum spumantibus aequoris undis
   subleuem et a mortis limine restituam,
quem neque sancta Venus molli requiescere somno   5
   desertum in lecto caelibe perpetitur,
nec ueterum dulci scriptorum carmine Musae
   oblectant, cum mens anxia peruigilat:
id gratum est mihi, me quoniam tibi dicis amicum,
   muneraque et Musarum hinc petis et Veneris.   10
sed tibi ne mea sint ignota incommoda, Mani,
   neu me odisse putes hospitis officium,
accipe, quis merser fortunae fluctibus ipse,
   ne amplius a misero dona beata petas.
tempore quo primum uestis mihi tradita pura est,   15
   iucundum cum aetas florida uer ageret,
multa satis lusi: non est dea nescia nostri,
   quae dulcem curis miscet amaritiem.
sed totum hoc studium luctu fraterna mihi mors
   abstulit. o misero frater adempte mihi,   20
tu mea tu moriens fregisti commoda, frater,
   tecum una tota est nostra sepulta domus,
omnia tecum una perierunt gaudia nostra,
   quae tuus in uita dulcis alebat amor.
cuius ego interitu tota de mente fugaui   25
   haec studia atque omnes delicias animi.
quare, quod scribis Veronae turpe Catullo
   esse, quod hic quisquis de meliore nota
frigida deserto tepefactet membra cubili,
   id, Mani, non est turpe, magis miserum est.   30

ignosces igitur si, quae mihi luctus ademit,
  haec tibi non tribuo munera, cum nequeo.
nam, quod scriptorum non magna est copia apud me,
  hoc fit, quod Romae uiuimus: illa domus,
illa mihi sedes, illic mea carpitur aetas; 35
  huc una ex multis capsula me sequitur.
quod cum ita sit, nolim statuas nos mente maligna
  id facere aut animo non satis ingenuo,
quod tibi non utriusque petenti copia posta est:
  ultro ego deferrem, copia siqua foret. 40

Allius has helped him nobly in his affair with Lesbia

Non possum reticere, deae, qua me Allius in re
  iuuerit aut quantis iuuerit officiis,
ne fugiens saeclis obliuiscentibus aetas
  illius hoc caeca nocte tegat studium:
sed dicam uobis, uos porro dicite multis 45
  milibus et facite haec carta loquatur anus.

. . . .

  notescatque magis mortuus atque magis,
nec tenuem texens sublimis aranea telam
  in deserto Alli nomine opus faciat. 50
nam, mihi quam dederit duplex Amathusia curam,
  scitis, et in quo me torruerit genere,
cum tantum arderem quantum Trinacria rupes
  lymphaque in Oetaeis Malia Thermopylis,
maesta neque assiduo tabescere lumina fletu 55
  cessarent tristique imbre madere genae.
qualis in aerii perlucens uertice montis
  riuus muscoso prosilit e lapide,
qui cum de prona praeceps est ualle uolutus,
  per medium densi transit iter populi, 60
dulce uiatori lasso in sudore leuamen,
  cum grauis exustos aestus hiulcat agros,
ac uelut in nigro iactatis turbine nautis
  lenius aspirans aura secunda uenit

iam prece Pollucis, iam Castoris implorata,   65
  tale fuit nobis Allius auxilium.
is clausum lato patefecit limite campum,
  isque domum nobis isque dedit dominae,
ad quam communes exerceremus amores.

Lesbia's love for Catullus reminds him of Laodamia's for Protesilaus

quo mea se molli candida diua pede   70
intulit et trito fulgentem in limine plantam
  innixa arguta constituit solea,
coniugis ut quondam flagrans aduenit amore
  Protesilaeam Laudamia domum
inceptam frustra, nondum cum sanguine sacro   75
  hostia caelestis pacificasset eros.
nil mihi tam ualde placeat, Ramnusia uirgo,
  quod temere inuitis suscipiatur eris.
quam ieiuna pium desideret ara cruorem,
  docta est amisso Laudamia uiro,   80
coniugis ante coacta noui dimittere collum,
  quam ueniens una atque altera rursus hiems
noctibus in longis auidum saturasset amorem,
  posset ut abrupto uiuere coniugio,
quod scibant Parcae non longo tempore abesse,   85
  si miles muros isset ad Iliacos.

Protesilaus died at Troy; so too did the poet's brother

nam tum Helenae raptu primores Argiuorum
  coeperat ad sese Troia ciere uiros,
Troia (nefas!) commune sepulcrum Asiae Europaeque,
  Troia uirum et uirtutum omnium acerba cinis,   90
quaene etiam nostro letum miserabile fratri
  attulit. ei misero frater adempte mihi,
ei misero fratri iucundum lumen ademptum,
  tecum una tota est nostra sepulta domus,
omnia tecum una perierunt gaudia nostra,   95
  quae tuus in uita dulcis alebat amor.

quem nunc tam longe non inter nota sepulcra
    nec prope cognatos compositum cineres,
sed Troia obscena, Troia infelice sepultum
    detinet extremo terra aliena solo.   100
ad quam tum properans fertur [lecta] undique **pubes**
    Graeca penetralis deseruisse focos,
ne Paris abducta gauisus libera moecha
    otia pacato degeret in thalamo.

When Protesilaus died, Laodamia's grief was profound, as her love was immeasurable

quo tibi tum casu, pulcerrima Laudamia,   105
    ereptum est uita dulcius atque anima
coniugium: tanto te absorbens uertice amoris
    aestus in abruptum detulerat barathrum,
quale ferunt Grai Pheneum prope Cyllenaeum
    siccare emulsa pingue palude solum,   110
quod quondam caesis montis fodisse medullis
    audit falsiparens Amphytrioniades,
tempore quo certa Stymphalia monstra sagitta
    perculit imperio deterioris eri,
pluribus ut caeli tereretur ianua diuis,   115
    Hebe nec longa uirginitate foret.
sed tuus altus amor barathro fuit altior illo,
    qui tamen indomitam ferre iugum docuit.
nam nec tam carum confecto aetate parenti
    una caput seri nata nepotis alit,   120
qui, cum diuitiis uix tandem inuentus auitis
    nomen testatas intulit in tabulas,
impia derisi gentilis gaudia tollens
    suscitat a cano uolturium capiti;
nec tantum niueo gauisa est ulla columbo   125
    compar, quae multo dicitur improbius
oscula mordenti semper decerpere rostro,
    quam quae praecipue multiuola est **mulier**.
sed tu horum magnos uicisti sola furores,
    ut semel es flauo conciliata uiro.   130

No less wonderful is Lesbia, despite her inconstancy
aut nihil aut paulo cui tum concedere digna
   lux mea se nostrum contulit in gremium,
quam circumcursans hinc illinc saepe Cupido
   fulgebat crocina candidus in tunica.
quae tamen etsi uno non est contenta Catullo,   135
   rara uerecundae furta feremus erae,
ne nimium simus stultorum more molesti.
   saepe etiam Iuno, maxima caelicolum,
coniugis in culpa flagrantem concoquit iram,
   noscens omniuoli plurima furta Iouis.   140
atqui nec diuis homines componier aequum est,

. . . .
. . . .

   ingratum tremuli tolle parentis onus.
nec tamen illa mihi dextra deducta paterna
   fragrantem Assyrio uenit odore domum,
sed furtiua dedit mira munuscula nocte,   145
   ipsius ex ipso dempta uiri gremio.
quare illud satis est, si nobis is datur unis
   quem lapide illa dies candidiore notat.

This is the best Catullus can do to show his gratitude to Allius.
May heaven bless the house where he met Lesbia!
hoc tibi, quod potui, confectum carmine munus
   pro multis, Alli, redditur officiis,   150
ne uestrum scabra tangat rubigine nomen
   haec atque illa dies atque alia atque alia.
huc addent diui quam plurima, quae Themis olim
   antiquis solita est munera ferre piis.
sitis felices et tu simul et tua uita,   155
   et domus ipsa in qua lusimus et domina,
et qui principio nobis †terram dedit aufert†,
   a quo sunt primo omnia nata bona,
et longe ante omnes mihi quae me carior ipso est,
   lux mea, qua uiua uiuere dulce mihi est.   160
LXVIII

62 Marriage Song (i)

The poet's offering to the bridal pair

He prays that Hymen will come and preside over the nuptials

COLLIS o Heliconii
cultor, Vraniae genus,
qui rapis teneram ad uirum
uirginem, o Hymenaee Hymen,
    o Hymen Hymenaee; 5

cinge tempora floribus
suaue olentis amaraci,
flammeum cape laetus, huc
huc ueni, niueo gerens
    luteum pede soccum; 10

excitusque hilari die,
nuptialia concinens
uoce carmina tinnula,
pelle humum pedibus, manu
    pineam quate taedam. 15

namque Iunia Manlio,
qualis Idalium colens
uenit ad Phrygium Venus
iudicem, bona cum bona
    nubit alite uirgo, 20

floridis uelut enitens
myrtus Asia ramulis
quos Hamadryades deae
ludicrum sibi roscido
    nutriunt umore. 25

quare age, huc aditum ferens,
perge linquere Thespiae
rupis Aonios specus,
nympha quos super irrigat
    frigerans Aganippe. 30

ac domum dominam uoca
coniugis cupidam noui,
mentem amore reuinciens,
ut tenax hedera huc et huc
   arborem implicat errans.   35

*He calls on the attendant maidens
to sing the god's praises*

uosque item simul, integrae
uirgines, quibus aduenit
par dies, agite in modum
dicite, o Hymenaee Hymen,
   o Hymen Hymenaee;   40

ut lubentius, audiens
se citarier ad suum
munus, huc aditum ferat
dux bonae Veneris, boni
   coniugator amoris.   45

quis deus magis est ama-
tis petendus amantibus?
quem colent homines magis
caelitum o Hymenaee Hymen,
   o Hymen Hymenaee?   50

te suis tremulus parens
inuocat, tibi uirgines
zonula soluunt sinus,
te timens cupida nouos
   captat aure maritus.   55

tu fero iuueni in manus
floridam ipse puellulam
dedis a gremio suae
matris, o Hymenaee Hymen,
   o Hymen Hymenaee.   60

nil potest sine te Venus,
fama quod bona comprobet,
commodi capere, at potest
te uolente. quis huic deo
   compararier ausit? 65

nulla quit sine te domus
liberos dare, nec parens
stirpe nitier; at potest
te uolente. quis huic deo
   compararier ausit? 70

quae tuis careat sacris,
non queat dare praesides
terra finibus: at queat
te uolente. quis huic deo
   compararier ausit? 75

*He assures the lovely bride
that she has nothing to fear*

claustra pandite ianuae.
uirgo adest. uiden ut faces
splendidas quatiunt comas?

. . . . . .

. . . . . .

. . . . . .
. . . . . .

tardet ingenuus pudor.
quem tamen magis audiens, 80
   flet quod ire necesse est.

flere desine. non tibi Au-
runculeia periculum est,
ne qua femina pulcrior
clarum ab Oceano diem 85
   uiderit uenientem.

talis in uario solet
diuitis domini hortulo
stare flos hyacinthinus.
sed moraris, abit dies. 90
    [prodeas noua nupta.]

prodeas noua nupta, si
iam uidetur, et audias
nostra uerba. uiden? faces
aureas quatiunt comas: 95
    prodeas noua nupta.

non tuus leuis in mala
deditus uir adultera,
probra turpia persequens,
a tuis teneris uolet 100
    secubare papillis,

lenta sed uelut adsitas
uitis impli at arbores,
implicabitur in tuum
complexum. sed abit dies: 105
    prodeas noua nupta.

o cubile, quod omnibus
  .   .   .   .   .
  .   .   .   .   .
  .   .   .   .   .
    candido pede lecti.

quae tuo ueniunt ero,
quanta gaudia, quae uaga 110
nocte, quae medio die
gaudeat! sed abit dies:
    prodeas noua nupta.

He bids the boys praise the god
yet more fervently as the bride
enters the bridegroom's house

tollite, [o] pueri, faces:
flammeum uideo uenire. 115
ite concinite in modum
'io Hymen Hymenaee io,
    io Hymen Hymenaee.'

en tibi domus ut potens
et beata uiri tui, 120
quae tibi sine seruiat,
(io Hymen Hymenaee io,
    io Hymen Hymenaee)

usque dum tremulum mouens
cana tempus anilitas 125
omnia omnibus annuit.
io Hymen Hymenaee io,
    io Hymen Hymenaee.

transfer omine cum bono
limen aureolos pedes, 130
rasilemque subi forem.
io Hymen Hymenaee io,
    io Hymen Hymenaee.

aspice intus ut accubans
uir tuus Tyrio in toro 135
totus immineat tibi.
io Hymen Hymenaee io,
    io Hymen Hymenaee.

illi non minus ac tibi
pectore uritur intimo 140
flamma, sed penite magis.
io Hymen Hymenaee io,
    io Hymen Hymenaee.

mitte brachiolum teres,
praetextate, puellulae: 145
iam cubile adeat uiri.

io Hymen Hymenaee io,
  io Hymen Hymenaee.

[uos] bonae senibus uiris
cognitae bene feminae
collocate puellulam.
io Hymen Hymenaee io,
  io Hymen Hymenaee.

*He invites the bridegroom to enter
the bridechamber, where countless
joys await him, and where he will
beget a son to delight his heart*

iam licet uenias, marite:
uxor in thalamo tibi est,
ore floridulo nitens,
alba parthenice uelut
  luteumue papauer.

at, marite, ita me iuuent
caelites, nihilo minus
pulcer es, neque te Venus
neglegit. sed abit dies:
  perge, ne remorare.

non diu remoratus es:
iam uenis. bona te Venus
iuuerit, quoniam palam
quod cupis cupis, et bonum
  non abscondis amorem.

ille pulueris Africi
siderumque micantium
subducat numerum prius,
qui uestri numerare uolt
  multa milia ludi.

ludite ut lubet, et breui
liberos date. non decet

tam uetus sine liberis
nomen esse, sed indidem
   semper ingenerari.

Torquatus uolo paruulus
matris e gremio suae   180
porrigens teneras manus
   dulce rideat ad patrem
      semihiante labello.

sit suo similis patri
Manlio et facile insciis   185
noscitetur ab omnibus,
   et pudicitiam suae
      matris indicet ore.

talis illius a bona
matre laus genus approbet,   190
qualis unica ab optima
   matre Telemacho manet
      fama Penelopeo.

claudite ostia, uirgines:
lusimus satis. at boni   195
coniuges, bene uiuite et
   munere assiduo ualentem
      exercete iuuentam.
LXI

63 MARRIAGE SONG (*ii*)

A colourful debate on the rival attractions of single and married blessedness

  The two sides prepare for the fray
VESPER adest, iuuenes, consurgite: **Vesper Olympo**
exspectata diu uix tandem lumina tollit.
surgere iam tempus, iam pinguis linquere **mensas,**
iam ueniet uirgo, iam dicetur **Hymenaeus.**
Hymen o Hymenaee, Hymen ades o Hymenaee!   5

Cernitis, innuptae, iuuenes? consurgite contra;
nimirum Oetaeos ostendit Noctifer ignes.
sic certest; uiden ut perniciter exsiluere?
non temere exsiluere, canent quod uincere par est.
Hymen o Hymenaee, Hymen ades o Hymenaee! 10

Non facilis nobis, aequales, palma parata est;
aspicite, innuptae secum ut meditata requirunt.
non frustra meditantur: habent memorabile quod sit;
nec mirum, penitus quae tota mente laborant.
nos alio mentes, alio diuisimus aures; 15
iure igitur uincemur: amat uictoria curam.
quare nunc animos saltem conuertite uestros;
dicere iam incipient, iam respondere decebit.
Hymen o Hymenaee, Hymen ades o Hymenaee!

The young women argue in favour of virginity:
the young men counter every argument

Hespere, quis caelo fertur crudelior ignis? 20
qui natam possis complexu auellere matris,
complexu matris retinentem auellere natam,
et iuueni ardenti castam donare puellam.
quid faciunt hostes capta crudelius urbe?
Hymen o Hymenaee, Hymen ades o Hymenaee! 25

Hespere, quis caelo lucet iucundior ignis?
qui desponsa tua firmes conubia flamma,
quae pepigere uiri, pepigerunt ante parentes,
nec iunxere prius quam se tuus extulit ardor.
quid datur a diuis felici optatius hora? 30
Hymen o Hymenaee, Hymen ades o Hymenaee!

Hesperus e nobis, aequales, abstulit unam.
. . . .
. . . .
namque tuo aduentu uigilat custodia semper;
nocte latent fures, quos idem saepe reuertens,
Hespere, mutato comprendis nomine Eous. 35

at lubet innuptis ficto te carpere questu.
quid tum, si carpunt, tacita quem mente requirunt?
Hymen o Hymenaee, Hymen ades o Hymenaee!

Vt flos in saeptis secretus nascitur hortis,
ignotus pecori, nullo conuolsus aratro, 40
quem mulcent aurae, firmat sol, educat imber;
multi illum pueri, multae optauere puellae:
idem cum tenui carptus defloruit ungui,
nulli illum pueri, nullae optauere puellae:
sic uirgo, dum intacta manet, dum cara suis est; 45
cum castum amisit polluto corpore florem,
nec pueris iucunda manet, nec cara puellis.
Hymen o Hymenaee, Hymen ades o Hymenaee!

Vt uidua in nudo uitis quae nascitur aruo,
numquam se extollit, numquam mitem educat uuam, 50
sed tenerum prono deflectens pondere corpus
iam iam contingit summum radice flagellum;
hanc nulli agricolae, nulli coluere iuuenci;
at si forte eadem est ulmo coniuncta marito,
multi illam agricolae, multi coluere iuuenci; 55
sic uirgo dum intacta manet, dum inculta senescit;
cum par conubium maturo tempore adepta est,
cara uiro magis et minus est inuisa parenti.
[Hymen o Hymenaee, Hymen ades o Hymenaee!]

Having won the debate the young men give good advice to the bride
Et tu ne pugna cum tali coniuge, uirgo.
non aequom est pugnare, pater cui tradidit ipse, 60
ipse pater cum matre, quibus parere necesse est.
uirginitas non tota tua est, ex parte parentum est,
tertia pars patrist, pars est data tertia matri,
tertia sola tua est: noli pugnare duobus,
qui genero sua iura simul cum dote dederunt. 65
Hymen o Hymenaee, Hymen ades o Hymenaee!

LXII

64 BERENICE'S LOCK

A playful piece of romantic nonsense

How the lock was sighted in the sky

OMNIA qui magni dispexit lumina mundi,
  qui stellarum ortus comperit atque obitus,
flammeus ut rapidi solis nitor obscuretur,
  ut cedant certis sidera temporibus,
ut Triuiam furtim sub Latmia saxa relegans   5
  dulcis amor gyro deuocet aereo:
idem me ille Conon caelesti in lumine uidit
  e Beroniceo uertice caesariem
fulgentem clare, quam multis illa dearum
  leuia protendens brachia pollicita est,   10
qua rex tempestate nouo auctus hymenaeo
  uastatum finis iuerat Assyrios,
dulcia nocturnae portans uestigia rixae,
  quam de uirgineis gesserat exuuiis.

How it came to be vowed to the goddess

estne nouis nuptis odio Venus? anne parentum   15
  frustrantur falsis gaudia lacrimulis,
ubertim thalami quas intra limina fundunt?
  non, ita me diui, uera gemunt, iuerint.
id mea me multis docuit regina querellis
  inuisente nouo proelia torua uiro.   20
et tu non orbum luxti deserta cubile,
  sed fratris cari flebile discidium?
quam penitus maestas exedit cura medullas!
  ut tibi tunc toto pectore sollicitae
sensibus ereptis mens excidit! at [te] ego certe   25
  cognoram a parua uirgine magnanimam.
anne bonum oblita es facinus, quo regium adepta es
  coniugium, quod non fortior ausit alis?
sed tum maesta uirum mittens quae uerba locuta es!
  Iuppiter, ut tristi lumina saepe manu!   30

quis te mutauit tantus deus? an quod amantes
    non longe a caro corpore abesse uolunt?
atque ibi me cunctis pro dulci coniuge diuis
    non sine taurino sanguine pollicita es,
si reditum tetulisset. is haut in tempore longo   35
    captam Asiam Aegypti finibus addiderat.
quis ego pro factis caelesti reddita coetu
    pristina uota nouo munere dissoluo.

How it was cut off and later placed among the stars

inuita, o regina, tuo de uertice cessi,
    inuita: adiuro teque tuumque caput,   40
digna ferat quod si quis inaniter adiurarit:
    sed qui se ferro postulet esse parem?
ille quoque euersus mons est, quem maximum in oris
    progenies Thiae clara superuehitur,
cum Medi peperere nouum mare, cumque iuuentus   45
    per medium classi barbara nauit Athon.
quid facient crines, cum ferro talia cedant?
    Iuppiter, ut Chalybon omne genus pereat,
et qui principio sub terra quaerere uenas
    institit ac ferri stringere duritiem!   50
abiunctae paulo ante comae mea fata sorores
    lugebant, cum se Memnonis Aethiopis
unigena impellens nutantibus aera pennis
    obtulit Arsinoes Locridos ales equos,
isque per aetherias me tollens auolat umbras   55
    et Veneris casto collocat in gremio.
ipsa suum Zephyritis eo famulum legarat,
    Graiia Canopitis incola litoribus.
†hi dii uen ibi† uario ne solum in lumine caeli
    ex Ariadnaeis aurea temporibus   60
fixa corona foret, sed nos quoque fulgeremus
    deuotae flaui uerticis exuuiae,
uuidulam a fluctu cedentem ad templa deum me
    sidus in antiquis diua nouum posuit.

Virginis et saeui contingens namque Leonis 65
    lumina, Callisto iuncta Lycaoniae,
uertor in occasum, tardum dux ante Booten,
    qui uix sero alto mergitur Oceano.

How distressed it felt

sed quamquam me nocte premunt uestigia diuum,
    lux autem canae Tethyi restituit, 70
(pace tua fari hic liceat, Ramnusia uirgo,
    namque ego non ullo uera timore tegam,
nec si me infestis discerpent sidera dictis,
    condita quin ueri pectoris euoluam)
non his tam laetor rebus, quam me afore semper, 75
    afore a dominae uertice discrucior,
quicum ego, dum uirgo quondam fuit omnibus expers
    unguentis, una uilia multa bibi.

*How glad it would be to receive offerings from chaste
wives; how much more glad to be a royal lock once more*

nunc uos, optato quas iunxit lumine taeda,
    non prius unanimis corpora coniugibus 80
tradite nudantes reiecta ueste papillas,
    quam iucunda mihi munera libet onyx,
uester onyx, casto colitis quae iura cubili.
    sed quae se impuro dedit adulterio,
illius a mala dona leuis bibat irrita puluis: 85
    namque ego ab indignis praemia nulla peto.
sed magis, o nuptae, semper concordia uestras,
    semper amor sedes incolat assiduus.
tu uero, regina, tuens cum sidera diuam
    placabis festis luminibus Venerem, 90
unguinis expertem non siris esse tuam me,
    sed potius largis affice muneribus.
sidera corruerint utinam! coma regia fiam,
    proximus Hydrochoi fulgeret Oarion!

LXVI

65 Attis

The story of a young man whom religious frenzy brought to destruction

How Attis unmanned himself and urged his companions to follow him to the haunts of Cybele

SVPER alta uectus Attis celeri rate maria,
Phrygium ut nemus citato cupide pede tetigit
adiitque opaca siluis redimita loca deae,
stimulatus ibi furenti rabie, uagus animis,
deuolsit ili acuto sibi pondera silice,   5
itaque ut relicta sensit sibi membra sine uiro,
etiam recente terrae sola sanguine maculans,
niueis citata cepit manibus leue typanum,
typanum tuum, Cybebe, tua, mater, initia,
quatiensque terga tauri teneris caua digitis   10
canere haec suis adorta est tremebunda comitibus.
'agite ite ad alta, Gallae, Cybeles nemora simul,
simul ite, Dindymenae dominae uaga pecora,
aliena quae petentes uelut exules loca
sectam meam exsecutae duce me mihi comites   15
rapidum salum tulistis truculentaque pelagi,
et corpus euirastis Veneris nimio odio;
hilarate erae citatis erroribus animum.
mora tarda mente cedat: simul ite, sequimini
Phrygiam ad domum Cybebes, Phrygia ad nemora deae,   20
ubi cymbalum sonat uox, ubi tympana reboant,
tibicen ubi canit Phryx curuo graue calamo,
ubi capita Maenades ui iaciunt hederigerae,
ubi sacra sancta acutis ululatibus agitant,
ubi sueuit illa diuae uolitare uaga cohors,   25
quo nos decet citatis celerare tripudiis.'

How the clamorous throng arrived exhausted

   simul haec comitibus Attis cecinit notha mulier,
thiasus repente linguis trepidantibus ululat,
leue tympanum remugit, caua cymbala recrepant,

LONGER POEMS 71

non flauo retinens subtilem uertice mitram,
non contecta leui uelatum pectus amictu,
non tereti strophio lactentis uincta papillas, 65
omnia quae toto delapsa e corpore passim
ipsius ante pedes fluctus salis alludebant.
sed neque tum mitrae neque tum fluitantis amictus
illa uicem curans toto ex te pectore, Theseu,
toto animo, tota pendebat perdita mente. 70
a misera, assiduis quam luctibus externauit
spinosas Erycina serens in pectore curas,
illa tempestate, ferox quo ex tempore Theseus
egressus curuis e litoribus Piraei
attigit iniusti regis Gortynia templa. 75

How Theseus had come to Crete, and how he had slain the Minotaur

nam perhibent olim crudeli peste coactam
Androgeoneae poenas exsoluere caedis
electos iuuenes simul ac decus innuptarum
Cecropiam solitam esse dapem dare Minotauro.
quis angusta malis cum moenia uexarentur, 80
ipse suum Theseus pro caris corpus Athenis
proicere optauit potius quam talia Cretam
funera Cecropiae nec funera portarentur.
atque ita naue leui nitens ac lenibus auris
magnanimum ad Minoa uenit sedesque superbas. 85
hunc simul ac cupido conspexit lumine uirgo
regia, quam suauis exspirans castus odores
lectulus in molli complexu matris alebat,
quales Eurotae praecingunt flumina myrtus
auraue distinctos educit uerna colores, 90
non prius ex illo flagrantia declinauit
lumina, quam cuncto concepit corpore flammam
funditus atque imis exarsit tota medullis.
heu misere exagitans immiti corde furores,
sancte puer, curis hominum qui gaudia misces, 95
quaeque regis Golgos quaeque Idalium frondosum,

72 POEMS OF CATULLUS

qualibus incensam iactastis mente puellam
fluctibus, in flauo saepe hospite suspirantem!
quantos illa tulit languenti corde timores!
quanto saepe magis fulgore expalluit auri, 100
cum saeuum cupiens contra contendere monstrum
aut mortem appeteret Theseus aut praemia laudis!
non ingrata tamen frustra munuscula diuis
promittens tacito succepit uota labello.
nam uelut in summo quatientem brachia Tauro 105
quercum aut conigeram sudanti cortice pinum
indomitus turbo contorquens flamine robur
eruit (illa procul radicitus exturbata
prona cadit, late quaeuis cumque obuia frangens),
sic domito saeuum prostrauit corpore Theseus 110
nequiquam uanis iactantem cornua uentis.
inde pedem sospes multa cum laude reflexit
errabunda regens tenui uestigia filo,
ne labyrintheis e flexibus egredientem
tecti frustraretur inobseruabilis error. 115

*How she had left her parents and accompanied him to Dia,
where he forsook her while she slept*

sed quid ego a primo digressus carmine plura
commemorem, ut linquens genitoris filia uultum,
ut consanguineae complexum, ut denique matris,
quae misera in gnata deperdita laeta[batur], 120
omnibus his Thesei dulcem praeoptarit amorem:
aut ut uecta rati spumosa ad litora Diae
[uenerit,] aut ut eam deuinctam lumina somno
liquerit immemori discedens pectore coniunx?
saepe illam perhibent ardenti corde furentem
clarisonas imo fudisse e pectore uoces, 125
ac tum praeruptos tristem conscendere montes,
unde aciem [in] pelagi uastos protenderet aestus,
tum tremuli salis aduersas procurrere in undas
mollia nudatae tollentem tegmina surae,
atque haec extremis maestam dixisse querellis, 130
frigidulos udo singultus ore cientem:

LONGER POEMS

How she charged him and all others of his sex with faithlessness and ingratitude

'sicine me patriis auectam, perfide, ab aris,
perfide, deserto liquisti in litore, Theseu?
sicine discedens neglecto numine diuum,
immemor a! deuota domum periuria portas?   135
nullane res potuit crudelis flectere mentis
consilium? tibi nulla fuit clementia praesto,
immite ut nostri uellet miserescere pectus?
at non haec quondam blanda promissa dedisti
uoce mihi, non haec miserae sperare iubebas,   140
sed conubia laeta, sed optatos hymenaeos,
quae cuncta aerii discerpunt irrita uenti.
nunc iam nulla uiro iuranti femina credat,
nulla uiri speret sermones esse fideles;
quis dum aliquid cupiens animus praegestit apisci,   145
nil metuunt iurare, nihil promittere parcunt:
sed simul ac cupidae mentis satiata libido est,
dicta nihil metuere, nihil periuria curant.
certe ego te in medio uersantem turbine leti
eripui, et potius germanum amittere creui,   150
quam tibi fallaci supremo in tempore dessem.
pro quo dilaceranda feris dabor alitibusque
praeda, neque iniacta tumulabor mortua terra.
quaenam te genuit sola sub rupe leaena,
quod mare conceptum spumantibus exspuit undis,   155
quae Syrtis, quae Scylla rapax, quae uasta Carybdis,
talia qui reddis pro dulci praemia uita?
si tibi non cordi fuerant conubia nostra,
saeua quod horrebas prisci praecepta parentis,
attamen in uestras potuisti ducere sedes,   160
quae tibi iucundo famularer serua labore,
candida permulcens liquidis uestigia lymphis,
purpureaue tuum consternens ueste cubile.
sed quid ego ignaris nequiquam conquerar auris,
externata malo, quae nullis sensibus auctae   165
nec missas audire queunt nec reddere uoces?

74 POEMS OF CATULLUS

ille autem prope iam mediis uersatur in undis,
nec quisquam apparet uacua mortalis in alga.
sic nimis insultans extremo tempore saeua
fors etiam nostris inuidit questibus auris. 170

*How in her hopeless situation she called down on im
the vengeance of heaven*

Iuppiter omnipotens, utinam ne tempore primo
Cnosia Cecropiae tetigissent litora puppes,
indomito nec dira ferens stipendia tauro
perfidus in Cretam religasset nauita funem,
nec malus hic celans dulci crudelia forma 175
consilia in nostris requiesset sedibus hospes!
nam quo me referam? quali spe perdita nitor?
Idaeosne petam montes? at gurgite lato
discernens ponti truculentum diuidit aequor.
an patris auxilium sperem? quemne ipsa reliqui 180
respersum iuuenem fraterna caede secuta?
coniugis an fido consoler memet amore?
quine fugit lentos incuruans gurgite remos?
praeterea nullo colitur sola insula tecto,
nec patet egressus pelagi cingentibus undis. 185
nulla fugae ratio, nulla spes: omnia muta,
omnia sunt deserta, ostentant omnia letum.
non tamen ante mihi languescent lumina morte,
nec prius a fesso secedent corpore sensus,
quam iustam a diuis exposcam prodita multam 190
caelestumque fidem postrema comprecer hora.
quare facta uirum multantes uindice poena
Eumenides, quibus anguino redimita capillo
frons exspirantis praeportat pectoris iras,
huc huc aduentate, meas audite querellas, 195
quas ego, uae misera, extremis proferre medullis
cogor inops, ardens, amenti caeca furore.
quae quoniam uerae nascuntur pectore ab imo,
uos nolite pati nostrum uanescere luctum,
sed quali solam Theseus me mente reliquit, 200
tali mente, deae, funestet seque suosque.'

LONGER POEMS

How the king of the gods fulfilled her prayer

has postquam maesto profudit pectore uoces,
supplicium saeuis exposcens anxia factis,
annuit inuicto caelestum numine rector;
quo motu tellus atque horrida contremuerunt   205
aequora concussitque micantia sidera mundus.
ipse autem caeca mentem caligine Theseus
consitus oblito dimisit pectore cuncta,
quae mandata prius constanti mente tenebat,
dulcia nec maesto sustollens signa parenti   210
sopitem Erectheum se ostendit uisere portum.
namque ferunt olim, classi cum moenia diuae
linquentem gnatum uentis concrederet Aegeus,
talia complexum iuueni mandata dedisse:
'gnate, mihi longa iucundior unice uita,   215
gnate, ego quem in dubios cogor dimittere casus,
reddite in extrema nuper mihi fine senectae,
quandoquidem fortuna mea ac tua feruida uirtus
eripit inuito mihi te, cui languida nondum
lumina sunt gnati cara saturata figura,   220
non ego te gaudens laetanti pectore mittam,
nec te ferre sinam fortunae signa secundae,
sed primum multas expromam mente querellas,
canitiem terra atque infuso puluere foedans,
inde infecta uago suspendam lintea malo,   225
nostros ut luctus nostraeque incendia mentis
carbasus obscurata dicet ferrugine Hibera.
quod tibi si sancti concesserit incola Itoni,
quae nostrum genus ac sedes defendere Erecthei
annuit, ut tauri respergas sanguine dextram,   230
tum uero facito ut memori tibi condita corde
haec uigeant mandata, nec ulla oblitteret aetas;
ut simul ac nostros inuisent lumina collis,
funestam antennae deponant undique uestem,
candidaque intorti sustollant uela rudentes,   235
quam primum cernens ut laeta gaudia mente
agnoscam, cum te reducem aetas prospera sistet.'

76 POEMS OF CATULLUS

haec mandata prius constanti mente tenentem
Thesea ceu pulsae uentorum flamine nubes
aereum niuei montis liquere cacumen.   240
at pater, ut summa prospectum ex arce petebat,
anxia in assiduos absumens lumina fletus,
cum primum infecti conspexit lintea ueli,
praecipitem sese scopulorum e uertice iecit,
amissum credens immiti Thesea fato.   245
sic funesta domus ingressus tecta paterna
morte ferox Theseus, qualem Minoidi luctum
obtulerat mente immemori, talem ipse recepit.
quae tum prospectans cedentem maesta carinam
multiplices animo uoluebat saucia curas.   250

How the coverlet portrayed Iacchus coming to woo her

at parte ex alia florens uolitabat Iacchus
cum thiaso Satyrorum et Nysigenis Silenis,
te quaerens, Ariadna, tuoque incensus amore.
. . . .
quae tum alacres passim lymphata mente furebant
euhoe bacchantes, euhoe capita inflectentes.   255
harum pars tecta quatiebant cuspide thyrsos,
pars e diuolso iactabant membra iuuenco,
pars sese tortis serpentibus incingebant,
pars obscura cauis celebrabant orgia cistis,
orgia quae frustra cupiunt audire profani,   260
plangebant aliae proceris tympana palmis,
aut tereti tenuis tinnitus aere ciebant;
multis raucisonos efflabant cornua bombos
barbaraque horribili stridebat tibia cantu.

*How, after feasting their eyes on the coverlet,
the human guests made way for the gods*

talibus amplifice uestis decorata figuris   265
puluinar complexa suo uelabat amictu.
quae postquam cupide spectando Thessala pubes
expleta est, sanctis coepit decedere diuis.

LONGER POEMS

hic, qualis flatu placidum mare matutino
horrificans Zephyrus procliuas incitat undas,
Aurora exoriente uagi sub limina Solis,
quae tarde primum clementi flamine pulsae
procedunt leuiterque sonant plangore cachinni,
post uento crescente magis magis increbescunt,
purpureaque procul nantes ab luce refulgent:
sic tum uestibuli linquentes regia tecta
ad se quisque uago passim pede discedebant.

How all the deities save two arrived with their gifts

quorum post abitum princeps e uertice Pelei
aduenit Chiron portans siluestria dona:
nam quoscumque ferunt campi, quos Thessala magnis
montibus ora creat, quos propter fluminis undas
aura parit flores tepidi fecunda Fauoni,
hos indistinctis plexos tulit ipse corollis,
quo permulsa domus iucundo risit odore.
confestim Penios adest, uiridantia Tempe,
Tempe, quae siluae cingunt super impendentes,
†Minosim linquens †doris celebranda choreis,
non uacuos: namque ille tulit radicitus altas
fagos ac recto proceras stipite laurus,
non sine nutanti platano lentaque sorore
flammati Phaethontis et aerea cupressu.
haec circum sedes late contexta locauit,
uestibulum ut molli uelatum fronde uireret.
post hunc consequitur sollerti corde Prometheus,
extenuata gerens ueteris uestigia poenae,
quam quondam silici restrictus membra catena
persoluit pendens e uerticibus praeruptis.
inde pater diuum sancta cum coniuge natisque
aduenit caelo, te solum, Phoebe, relinquens
unigenamque simul cultricem montibus Idri:
Pelea nam tecum pariter soror aspernata est,
nec Thetidis taedas uoluit celebrare iugalis.

78 POEMS OF CATULLUS

How during the wedding-feast the Fates chanted the destiny of the bridal pair

qui postquam niueis flexerunt sedibus artus,
large multiplici constructae sunt dape mensae,
cum interea infirmo quatientes corpora motu
ueridicos Parcae coeperunt edere cantus.   305
his corpus tremulum complectens undique uestis
candida purpurea talos incinxerat ora,
at roseae niueo residebant uertice uittae,
aeternumque manus carpebant rite laborem.   310
laeua colum molli lana retinebat amictum,
dextera tum leuiter deducens fila supinis
formabat digitis, tum prono in pollice torquens
libratum tereti uersabat turbine fusum,
atque ita decerpens aequabat semper opus dens, 315
laneaque aridulis haerebant morsa labellis,
quae prius in leui fuerant exstantia filo:
ante pedes autem candentis mollia lanae
uellera uirgati custodibant calathisci.
haec tum clarisona pellentes uellera uoce   320
talia diuino fuderunt carmine fata,
carmine, perfidiae quod post nulla arguet aetas.

How the bride would bear her beloved husband a son, Achilles, the greatest of warriors, who would destroy the Trojans

o decus eximium magnis uirtutibus augens,
Emathiae tutamen, Opis carissime nato,
accipe, quod laeta tibi pandunt luce sorores,
ueridicum oraclum: sed uos, quae fata sequuntur, 325
currite ducentes subtegmina, currite, fusi.
adueniet tibi iam portans optata maritis
Hesperus, adueniet fausto cum sidere coniunx,
quae tibi flexanimo mentem perfundat amore,
languidulosque paret tecum coniungere somnos, 330
leuia substernens robusto brachia collo.
currite ducentes subtegmina, currite, fusi.
nulla domus tales umquam contexit amores,

LONGER POEMS

nullus amor tali coniunxit foedere amantes, 335
qualis adest Thetidi, qualis concordia Peleo.
    currite ducentes subtegmina, currite, fusi.
nascetur uobis expers terroris Achilles,
hostibus haud tergo, sed forti pectore notus,
qui persaepe uago uictor certamine cursus 340
flammea praeuertet celeris uestigia ceruae.
    currite ducentes subtegmina, currite, fusi.
non illi quisquam bello se conferet heros,
cum Phrygii Teucro manabunt sanguine [campi,]
Troicaque obsidens longinquo moenia bello, 345
periuri Pelopis uastabit tertius heres.
    currite ducentes subtegmina, currite, fusi.
illius egregias uirtutes claraque facta
saepe fatebuntur gnatorum in funere matres,
cum incultum cano soluent a uertice crinem, 350
putridaque infirmis uariabunt pectora palmis.
    currite ducentes subtegmina, currite, fusi.
namque uelut densas praecerpens messor aristas
sole sub ardenti flauentia demetit arua,
Troiugenum infesto prosternet corpora ferro. 355
    currite ducentes subtegmina, currite, fusi.
testis erit magnis uirtutibus unda Scamandri,
quae passim rapido diffunditur Hellesponto,
cuius iter caesis angustans corporum aceruis
alta tepefaciet permixta flumina caede. 360
    currite ducentes subtegmina, currite, fusi.
denique testis erit morti quoque reddita praeda,
cum teres excelso coaceruatum aggere bustum
excipiet niueos perculsae uirginis artus.
    currite ducentes subtegmina, currite, fusi. 365
nam simul ac fessis dederit fors copiam Achiuis
urbis Dardaniae Neptunia soluere uincla,
alta Polyxenia madefient caede sepulcra;
quae, uelut ancipiti succumbens uictima ferro,
proiciet truncum summisso poplite corpus. 370
    currite ducentes subtegmina, currite, fusi.

80   POEMS OF CATULLUS

quare agite optatos animi coniungite amores.
accipiat coniunx felici foedere diuam,
dedatur cupido iam-dudum nupta marito.
    currite ducentes subtegmina, currite, fusi.   375
non illam nutrix orienti luce reuisens
hesterno collum poterit circumdare filo,   377
anxia nec mater discordis maesta puellae   379
secubitu caros mittet sperare nepotes.   380
    currite ducentes subtegmina, currite, fusi.

*How it was the custom of the gods to pay such visits to men,
until human wickedness banished them from human sight*

talia praefantes quondam felicia Pelei
carmina diuino cecinerunt pectore Parcae.
praesentes namque ante domos inuisere castas
heroum, et sese mortali ostendere coetu,
caelicolae nondum spreta pietate solebant.   385
saepe pater diuum templo in fulgente reuisens,
annua cum festis uenissent sacra diebus,
conspexit terra centum procumbere tauros.
saepe uagus Liber Parnasi uertice summo   390
Thyiadas effusis euantis crinibus egit,
cum Delphi tota certatim ex urbe ruentes
acciperent laeti diuum fumantibus aris.
saepe in letifero belli certamine Mauors
aut rapidi Tritonis era aut Amarunsia uirgo   395
armatas hominum est praesens hortata cateruas.
sed postquam tellus scelere est imbuta nefando
iustitiamque omnes cupida de mente fugarunt,
perfudere manus fraterno sanguine fratres,
destitit exstinctos gnatus lugere parentes,   400
optauit genitor primaeui funera nati,
liber ut innuptae poteretur flore nouercae,
ignaro mater substernens se impia nato
impia non uerita est diuos scelerare penates.

*Justice has left the world (398+406) ∴ Gods don't show themselves to this evil world any more.
Something has happened for Catullus to write this — see poem 11 ★*

LONGER POEMS 81

good and evil
omnia **fanda nefanda** malo permixta furore   405
iustificam nobis mentem auertere deorum.
quare nec talis dignantur uisere coetus, — *brings us back to marriage of Peleus and Thetis.*
nec se contingi patiuntur lumine claro.

*←type
compound adjective*

LXIV
not a very optimistic ending.

Positive: Prometheus
Negative: Five ages of man
   Hesiod - Greek poet.
   (Golden, Silver, Heroic, Bronze, us.)
as time progresses, "man's worth" decreases.

— Aratus (Hellenistic/Alexandrian poet) talks about how things got worse after Goddess justice left earth.

★+ when Theseus was immemor (negligent) which hurt Ariadne — it's like the plough in poem 11 hurting Catullus the flower with its carelessness.

NOTES

1

A dedication presumably written last and prefixed to selected poems. For the Hendecasyllabic metre see Appendix II.

1 **dono:** A colloquial substitute for the deliberative subjunctive, used also by Vergil. So we say 'Where do I go next?' **nouum:** Not 'my new book', which would imply that it was not his first. Catullus means that it is only now being published. Perhaps 'brand-new'. **libellum:** This cannot refer to the whole book that we possess, which is too long to be called a *libellus* or to be inscribed on a single roll; nor could the longer poems be called *nugae*.

2 **pumice:** used for polishing the ends of the roll.

3 **Corneli:** Cornelius Nepos, historian, biographer and poet. His *'Lives'* alone survive. We cannot say whether the next poem is addressed to the same man.

6 Nepos had written a history of the world in three scholarly volumes.

8 **quicquid hoc libelli qualecumque:** 'this humble little book, such as it is'. The reading is doubtful.

9–10 **Patrona uirgo:** the poet's special muse. **quod maneat:** a wish (jussive subjunctive). *quod* must be translated 'it'.

2

1 **si quicquam:** See note on 7.1. Here better translated 'if anything has ever ...'. **tacito:** antecedent to *cuius*. Bring them together—'to one with sealed lips whose faithful heart (or 'loyalty of heart') is known through and through'. Be careful to translate *fido* and *fides* correspondingly: both friends are equally faithful, loyal, or trustworthy.

3 **meque:** According to some scholars -*que* = *quoque*; according to others it means 'both' (which is better omitted in translating), -*que* and *et* being a not uncommon combination; according to yet others the text is corrupt.

illorum iure sacratum: 'bound by their code' (Fordyce). *illorum* means the *tacitus* and the *fidus amicus*.

4 **puta:** 'you must think'. The balancing of an imperative against an indicative (*inuenies*) is not found elsewhere in Latin, and is not permissible in English.

Arpocratem: The Greek name for the child Horus, often represented in Egypt as a baby touching his mouth with his finger, as babies do, and misunderstood in Rome as the god of silence. So Varro, writing soon after Catullus—*Arpocrates digito significat ut taceam*.

3

1 **Verani:** Veranius and Fabullus were on the governor's staff together in Spain, and later, it seems, in Macedonia. Nothing more is known about them.

2 **antistans:** 'worth more'.

3 **tuos penates:** literally 'your store-cupboard gods'. Translate 'your own hearth'.

4 **unanimos:** not 'unanimous' but 'loving'. You will meet this word again. **anum:** Noun used adjectivally, as elsewhere.

5 **nuntii beati:** Exclamations of this sort are usually in the accusative, but in 66 Catullus has *a misera*, and there are instances in Cicero.

6 **Hiberum:** genitive plural, the original decl. 2 form, 'of the Iberians'.

7 **nationes:** always used of primitive peoples.

8 **applicans:** 'drawing towards me'.

10 **iucundum:** 'beloved' or 'dear'. See note on 23.16. **quantum . . . beatiorum:** 'of all the lucky men alive'. For the partitive genitive compare 1.8. The comparative need not be pressed.

11 **quid:** 'who'. So Cicero writes of his brother *nihil mitius*—'no one could be gentler'.

4

1-3 **mi:** a word reserved for intimate friends. Distinguish the vocative of *meus* from the dative of *ego*, which we shall meet in 34.5 and 36.1.

cenabis . . . fauent . . . attuleris: Observe the careful choice of tenses: Fabullus will dine well if the gods (habitually) are kind to him, and if (before the dinner) he brings plenty of food.

4 **non sine:** more than *cum*—'and, needless to say, a pretty girl'.

NOTES   85

5 **sale:** not 'salt' but (as often) 'wit'. **omnibus:** 'every kind of'.

6 **uenuste noster:** 'my charming friend'.

9 **contra:** 'in return'. **meros amores:** 'the quintessence of love'.

10 **seu quid ... est:** 'or anything else that is ...'.

11 **unguentum:** really ointment, but better translated 'perfume'.

12 **Veneres Cupidinesque:** 'the Venuses and Cupids' or 'the deities of love and desire'.

13 **quod:** Be careful always to distinguish the neuter relative (as here) from the conjunction. Translate (as often) 'this'.

14 **totum:** agrees with *te*, but translate 'all nose'.

5

Varus, who cannot be identified, assumed that his friend had enriched himself abroad in the normal way.

1 **amores:** Catullus regularly uses this word combined with a possessive adjective to mean 'beloved', 'lady-love'.

2 **uisum:** When can purpose be expressed by the supine? **e foro otiosum:** 'from the forum where I was idling'.

3 **scortillum:** 'a little hussy'. Note that there are some neuter nouns which denote persons. In poem 6 Catullus calls Calvus *salaputium*, and Cicero calls Verres *acroama* 'entertainer'.

repente: 'at a glance'. The clause refers not to *scortillum* but to the description in the next line, which means 'certainly not lacking in wit or charm'. Note the frequent use of these adjectives and of the corresponding affirmative forms.

5 **ut:** 'as soon as', a common meaning when used with perfect indicative, especially in Vergil.

6–7 **quid ... Bithynia:** 'what was happening in Bithynia, how it was getting on'. Both idioms are used by Cicero.

8 **et aere:** 'and how much it had been worth to me in hard cash'.

9 **neque:** 'either'. *neque* after *nemo*, *nihil*, and other negatives must be translated affirmatively. Otherwise two negatives cancel out.

10 **cohors:** officially a governor's 'staff': but his fortune-hunting hangers-on are included.

11 **cur:** relative, not interrogative. In English we can say 'no

reason why' but not 'nothing why'; so translate 'whereby', or perhaps 'to enable'.

caput ... referret: literally 'bring his head back more oiled'. Perhaps 'return any the richer'.

12 **quibus esset:** causal subjunctive; but translate 'when they had'.

13 **non faceret pili:** 'who did not care two pins for'. Look up *pilus*, and distinguish from *pilum*.

14 **at certe tamen:** 'but surely at least'. **quod:** i.e. *id quod*, explained by *ad ... homines*.

14-15 **illic natum:** 'a native product'. The *lectica octophorus* originated in Bithynia. See line 20.

16 **ad lecticam homines:** 'litter-bearers'.

17 'make myself out to be extra lucky'.

18 **non mihi ... maligne:** 'I wasn't so hard up'.

19 **incidisset:** 'had fallen to my lot'.

20 **parare:** = *comparare* of line 15. **rectos:** as usual, not a participle but an adjective—'with straight backs'.

21 **hic ... illic:** Do not translate 'here ... there'. Name the places.

22 **grabati:** a colloquial word in keeping with the tone of the whole poem. There is no real English equivalent; perhaps 'pallet' or 'truckle-bed' might do.

24 **hic:** 'hereupon', 'at this', as often in Vergil. **ut ... cinaediorem:** 'as you'd expect of such a shameless creature'.

26 **commoda:** The short final vowel of the imperative is colloquial. **ad Serapim:** 'to the temple of Serapis', presumably to seek a cure: Serapis was a god of healing, imported from Egypt.

27 **mane:** See note on *commoda* above, and compare *caue* in 23.18. Notice the hiatus at the pause. **inquii:** Only here.

28 This line may be adverbial—'As for my saying I had them' (Fordyce), or 'As to what I said I had'; or it may be the object of *parauit* (Simpson), the intervening clauses being excited interruptions.

modo: See the vocabulary.

29 **fugit me ratio:** 'I made a slip'.

30 **Cinna:** C. Helvius Cinna ('Cinna the poet' in Shakespeare's *Julius Caesar*).

31 **quid ad me:** 'What's that to me?'

32 **tam bene quam:** Understand *si*, as frequently after *tamquam*, and translate *pararim* (which is normal) by a pluperfect.

33 **male:** This word ('very') and *uiuis* ('you are') are colloquial.

34 **per . . . neglegentem:** 'who won't let me speak carelessly', or more freely 'who insist on my weighing every word'.

6

C. Licinius Calvus, the most eminent after Catullus of the *noui poetae* and his closest friend, was both poet and orator. In physique he was diminutive, but his energy was enormous and his verbal onslaughts extremely fierce. His speeches against Vatinius became models pored over by student orators a century and more later.

1 **nescio quem:** Unless followed by the subjunctive of an indirect question *nescio quis* means 'somebody'. **corona:** Roman trials took place in the open forum, and the crowd which gathered round (hence the word *corona*) were allowed to applaud and to make audible comments.

2 **mirifice:** one of Catullus' favourite colloquialisms. **Vatiniana:** Do not use an adjective in English for this or any similar word.

3 **crimina:** not 'crimes' but 'accusations', 'charges'. **Caluos:** Note for future reference the spelling of such nominatives.

4 **admirans, manus tollens:** Both express a combination of surprise and admiration.

5 **salaputium:** found only here. We may keep the order by translating 'My goodness! The little chap can talk!'

7

Catullus touchingly and with tasteful brevity acknowledges receipt of the elegy which Calvus had written on the death of his young wife, and in which he seems to have confessed with regret that he had been unfaithful to her. Both poets wrote in the Elegiac metre. See Appendix II.

1-2 **si quicquam:** An emphatic but not unusual substitute for *si quid*—'if anything at all'. **mutis:** 'silent'. **acceptum:** 'acceptable'. So *inuictus* 'invincible'. **sepulcris:** dative to be taken with both *gratum acceptumue* and *accidere*, which means not 'happen' but 'reach', as in Livy's *auribus accidere*.

2-3 **dolore, quo desiderio:** In modern English we do not use the relative as an adjective. Translate 'grief, the longing with which . . .' and cf. Caesar's *Arduennae, quae silua* 'the Ardennes, a forest which . . .'.

3-4 **amores, amicitias:** two words for the same thing. So in poem 43, where, as here, we must not translate the second word as 'friendship'. Perhaps 'affection', though the Latin is much stronger. The two plurals are justified by *renouamus*: Catullus is perhaps thinking of his own love-affairs as well as Calvus's.

missas: Most editors translate 'lost' (= *amissas*), but quote no other instance of this meaning. Fordyce rightly says that the word implies voluntary abandonment. This meaning is common; the word often has the same meaning as *dimittere*, and Cicero writes *amicitiam dimittere*. Translate 'the affection we once threw away'.

5 **certe:** 'assuredly'.

8

1-2 **malest:** Such compression is common in early Latin poetry. It is impossible to say whether Catullus was sick in body or sick at heart, or whether in the first case this was his last illness, or in the second his grief was due to the break with Lesbia.

Cornifici: Probably Q. Cornificius, a successful general and a *nouus poeta*.

3 'and that more and more every day and every hour'. *cotidie* is not used with comparatives.

4-5 'And you—though it is the smallest and easiest task—with what word of comfort have you consoled him?' Retain both the emphatic *tu* and the deliberately broken flow of the words.

6 **sic meos amores:** either 'Is that how my dear friend behaves?' or 'Is that how you reward my affection?' The use of the plural is against the second interpretation. See note on 5.1.

7 'Just one little word of comfort.'

8 **Simonideis:** Simonides was a Greek lyric poet, greatly admired for the pathos of his elegies.

9

Catullus reproaches a former friend who has come between Lesbia and himself.

1 **non ideo sperabam:** 'not for this reason did I hope'. The reason is explained in lines 3-4. **Gelli:** probably L. Gellius

Poplicola, who later fought for Antony against Octavian. He is believed to have been a member of Clodius' circle.

2 perdito: 'desperate', as in 58.3.

3 nossem, putarem: subjunctives of rejected reason.

5 usu: 'familiar friendship'.

7 duxti: 'you thought'. Note the compressed form. Vergil does the same with other verbs, perhaps reproducing the everyday pronunciation, like 'don't' for 'do not'.

8 quaecumque: *cumque*, which duplicates *omni*, may be disregarded.

10

Catullus has tried in vain to make peace with Gellius: now it is to be *combat à l'outrance*, a threat which he carried out by hurling at his enemy's head five unprintable poems.

3 tibi: Where the thing sent is a gift, *mitto* often takes the dative rather than *ad* with the accusative.

studioso ... uenante: An adjective is similarly combined with a present participle in several passages of Vergil, e.g. *tenuis fugiens riuus* and *saxosus sonans Hypanis*, both in *Georgic* iv. Here the force of the adjective is more definitely adverbial, and it should be so translated.

requirens: equivalent to *quamquam* with a past tense, enabling historic sequence to be used in lines 2-3, although the main verb that follows is present. Translate either 'Although I have often sought ... now I see ...', or 'I have often sought ... but now I see ...'.

2 uti: 'how'. **Battiadae:** 'Battus' son'. Callimachus, the Alexandrian poet (born *c*. 310 B.C.) is meant, but names should rarely be altered in translating.

3 A line without one dactyl. The only parallel is in Ennius. To accord with the meaning of the line Catullus has achieved the utmost smoothness.

qui: an old ablative, which (like *quo* in a final clause containing a comparative), though originally a relative, became a conjunction and invariable. **lenirem:** 'make you more gentle'.

4 in usque caput: 'full in my face'.

6 hic ualuisse: 'have availed nothing in this'.

7 contra: 'in reply'. The line as it stands cannot be scanned, and *amitha* has no known meaning. Among many emendations the favourite is *euitamus amictu* 'I parry with my cloak'; but the future is required, and the safest thing is to omit *amitha* in translating.

8 **fixus:** equivalent to *transfixus*, as often in other poets.

dabis: In earlier times final *s* had been so lightly pronounced that it could be disregarded at will by poets from Ennius to Cicero and Lucretius. Catullus takes the liberty nowhere but here, and his successors abandoned it altogether.

11

1 **de quoquam quicquam bene mereri:** 'to deserve any good of anyone'. **uelle:** as often in Catullus, 'seek', 'try'.

2 **aliquem:** not 'anyone' but 'someone'.

3 **ingrata:** 'unrequited'.

4 **magis:** 'rather'.

6 Observe the rhythm of this line, which with its trisyllabic ending and five elisions (one of them at the caesura) breaks all the Ovidian rules, but is the perfect expression of a grief that chokes the poet.

12

A rebuke to a friend (perhaps the same person as Varus) who had shown the disloyalty which always cut Catullus to the heart. His emotions are perfectly conveyed by the slow broken rhythm of the Choriambic metre, for which see Appendix II.

1 **immemor:** not 'forgetful' but 'faithless' or 'ungrateful', like Theseus in poem 66.

2 **dulcis amiculi:** 'poor once-cherished friend'.

4 **nec:** 'and yet'.

5 **quae:** 'this truth'. The antecedent is not *facta* but the substance of line 4.

6 **faciant . . . habeant:** deliberative questions, direct if the punctuation is correct.

10 **uentos . . . nebulas:** subjects of *ferre*; but preserve the order by making them instruments with an English passive.

11 **at:** 'yet', not 'but'.

13

1 **mala mens**: a common expression for 'madness', as *bona mens* is for the opposite. **miselle**: in mock pity—'you poor creature'.

Rauide: Presumably the actual name of one of Catullus' rivals for Lesbia's favours. As it is a harmless word meaning 'grey', it can hardly be an abusive substitute, and Catullus seems never to have concealed the names of his enemies. Note that it is scanned as a dissyllable. Hypermeter (an extra syllable elided before an initial vowel in the next line) is found nowhere else in hendecasyllables; so we can safely pronounce the name as if spelt *Raude*. Plautus' pun on *auidi* and *audi* provides an exact parallel.

2 **iambos**: not 'iambics' but 'lampoons'.

3 **quis**: The common belief that *quis* is the pronoun and *qui* the adjective is false. *quis* is the predominant form for both parts of speech; *quis deus* is very common indeed. For *qui* as a pronoun see note on 59.22.

non bene aduocatus: either 'invoked to your harm' (because it was bad for you to have your prayer answered), or more probably 'invoked in the wrong way' (so that the god was annoyed and took revenge on you). See note on 60.21-4.

5 'Or [are you doing this] in order to make yourself talked about by the mob?'; or simply 'Or do you *want* to be the object of common talk?'

6 **quid uis**: 'What are you after?' See note on 11.1. **qualubet**: 'at all costs'.

7 **meos amores**: See note on 5.1.

8 **cum longa poena**: 'to your everlasting punishment'. For this use of *cum* cf. Caesar's *magno cum periculo equitum*.

14

Though Caesar had been his father's friend and he was willing to praise him as a conqueror, Catullus disliked him as a man and poured scorn upon him.

1 **uelle**: See note on 11.1.

2 **albus an ater homo**: Beware of translating 'a white or a black man', which conveys an utterly false meaning. Nor must it be translated 'fair or dark'. The expression is a colloquialism used also by Cicero. The poet means 'I don't want to know the first thing about you'.

15

A fragment of a lost poem.

1 Scan *irascere*. **iambis:** See note on 13.2.

2 **unice:** not 'unique', which would be complimentary, but 'one and only', which is sarcastic.

16

Catullus was fond of contrasting those he admired with those he did not. See also 17, 29, 30, 41, 42. Here he contrasts two scoundrels who had grown rich while serving abroad under Piso with two worthies who had not.

1 **duae sinistrae:** The left hand was regarded as the thieving hand. Why does Catullus insert *duae*? Surely because in the literal sense Piso had only one; editors have found a non-existent difficulty here.

2 **Pisonis:** probably L. Calpurnius Piso, Caesar's father-in-law, whose conduct as proconsul of Macedonia was scathingly attacked by Cicero. **scabies famesque:** nouns best translated by adjectives—'itching and hungry for . . .'.

mundi: objective genitive. It is generally taken here to mean 'the world', but this meaning is not found earlier than Horace. See note on 64.1, and translate 'sky'.

4 **Priapus:** Retain the word, or substitute 'monster of lust'. Use a passive as in 12.10. Priapus was a god of fertility imported from the Hellespont. See *Georgic* iv, 111 and Horace, *Satires I* viii.

6 **de die:** 'during working hours'.

7 **quaerunt in triuio:** 'beg at the street corner for . . .'.

17

1 **Marrucine Asini:** Reverse the names; when the *praenomen* was omitted, the *nomen* was often placed after the *cognomen*, e.g. *Caesar Iulius*. **manu sinistra:** See note on 16.1.

2 Most editors put the stop after *in ioco atque uino*; but adverbial phrases should if possible be taken with the verb which follows.

belle: a colloquial word, frequent in Cicero's letters. We have the adjective (which Catullus prefers to *pulcer*) in 42.14-15.

3 In another poem Catullus tells us that among other things his cloak was stolen. Martial was later to complain more than once of the prevalence of petty thefts. **neglegentiorum:** 'of men at

all careless'. Catullus is fond of ending a hendecasyllabic line with such comparatives. We might substitute 'of guests caught off their guard'.

4 **salsum**: 'funny' or 'a clever joke'. **fugit te:** 'you're sadly mistaken'.

5 **quamuis:** here not a conjunction 'although' but an adverb—literally 'as you wish'. Put it at the end of the sentence and translate it 'as can be'; or translate the whole line 'It is an utterly shabby trick in the worst taste'.

6 **Pollioni:** C. Asinius Pollio, later the friend of Vergil and Horace, and an eminent advocate, historian, and poet.

7 **uel:** 'even'.

8 **mutari:** *muto* occasionally means to undo something already done. We might translate the clause 'who would gladly give a whole talent to have your theft wiped out'. A talent was worth more than £1000 in present-day values.

9–10 **leporum differtus ac facetiarum:** The MSS read *disertus*, which seems impossible with the genitives. These cannot be taken with *puer*, as a descriptive genitive must have an epithet. Moreover while Pollio's *lepores* and *facetiae* contrast admirably with Marrucinus' attempts to be *salsus*, there is no point in referring to his fluency as a speaker. *differtus* gives excellent sense, and the genitives are those commonly used with *plenus*.

puer: If the poem was written before Catullus went to Bithynia, Pollio cannot have been more than eighteen.

14–15 It is essential to retain Catullus' order by substituting a passive verb. **ex Hiberis:** Latin often names the people where we name the place. **Saetaba:** 'Saetaban', i.e. from Saetabus in Hispania Tarraconensis.

15–17 Note the care with which Catullus emphasises the equality of esteem in which he holds his two friends. Having put Fabullus before Veranius he repeats the names in reverse order: and as Fabullus gets extra attention by providing the last word of the poem, Veranius gets extra by the use of an affectionate diminutive and the addition of *meum*. It is a matter, not of metrical convenience but of superlative skill. Cf. Shakespeare's 'All hail, Macbeth and Banquo; Banquo and Macbeth, all hail', and the similarly tactful address to Rosencrantz and Gildenstern. Observe also that in line 13 with *mei sodalis* Catullus treats them as a single person, just as in 36 he treats the twin gods Castor and Pollux.

18

Egnatius, long-haired, bearded, and displaying his dazzling teeth in a permanent grin, was, as we are told in another savage lampoon, prominent among Lesbia's lovers. For the metre (Scazon or Choliambic) see Appendix II.

2 **usque quaque:** 'wherever he goes'. **rei:** not from *res*.

8–10 **urbanum:** 'in good taste'; in line 10 'a city man'. Or, in order to link the two, we might translate 'worthy of a Roman' and 'a Roman'. The names that follow are carefully arranged to lead from the capital towards Spain.

monendum est te: a very rare alternative for *tu monendus es*; but Lucretius has *poenas timendum est* and several similar expressions.

11 **pinguis, obesus:** The second epithet is much stronger than the first. The MSS read *parcus* 'stingy', but a physical description is required, and *pinguis* is found in an ancient comment on this passage.

12 **dentatus:** 'toothy'.

14 **puriter:** See note on 54.19. Here Catullus is perhaps imitating the language of ceremonial cleansings. **lauit:** from *lauere*, a rare alternative for *lauare*.

17 **nunc:** 'in actual fact'. **Celtiber:** The Celtiberians were a mixture of Celts and Iberians in Spain.

18 **minxit:** perhaps 'has passed in the night'.

20 **ut:** consecutive. **uester:** Here and in a very few other passages *uester* seems to be equivalent to *tuus*, though *uos* is never equivalent to *tu*.

20–21 **quo ... hoc:** the same as *quanto ... tanto*. **loti:** We might paraphrase 'the filthy stuff'.

19

It may seem snobbery to treat with scorn a person whose pronunciation is not that heard in the best circles, but Catullus condemns Arrius not for ignorance but for a family affectation on which he prides himself, as is evident from lines 3–4. An Englishman is more likely to be derided for dropping aitches than for inserting them; but it can be disastrous for him if he mispronounces 'honest'. In Catullus' time even educated Romans were puzzled about the right places to sound aspirates, whether with vowels or with consonants, and fashion was inconstant.

NOTES

1–2 With a little ingenuity *chommoda* and *hinsidias* can be kept in the places where Catullus has purposely put them. Notice that he has chosen words to illustrate the aspiration of both consonants and vowels. For *chommoda* Simpson suggests 'whinnings', but this is a mistake no Englishman would make, and it is perhaps better to write 'hextras' or 'hadvantages'.

si quando uellet dicere: 'whenever he meant'. The subjunctive denotes indefinite frequency, as occasionally in prose. Cf. 65.67, *linquendum ubi esset cubiculum*.

3–4 tum ... cum: 'every time that'. Notice the indicative *dixerat*, normal when *cum* means 'whenever'. **sperabat:** 'prided himself'. **quantum poterat:** 'with all his lung-power'. As before, keep *hinsidias* last. **credo:** 'I suppose', as commonly in Cicero when not used as a main verb.

5 sic: 'that was how ...'.

mater: The Greeks and Romans believed that a woman acquired the accents of her parents and passed them on to her children without alteration, but there must be some other reason why the uncle is brought in. One difficulty is that we do not know whether to write *liber* or *Liber*. Nowhere else is *Liber* the name of a man, but always a complimentary alternative for *Bacchus*. If *liber* is right, it perhaps implies that the uncle was the only free member of the family; but this is very unconvincing. The text may be corrupt, but we cannot emend it.

7 requierant: for *requieuerant* 'had a holiday'. **omnibus:** 'everyone's'.

8 audibant: so *custodibant* in 66.319; an old form used by Vergil also. **leniter:** 'spoken smoothly'.

9 talia uerba: Most translators take this as the object and tend to neglect the awkward *sibi*. We might paraphrase *nec sibi metuebant* as 'and were not afraid of hearing'. But it is surely better to take *talia uerba* as the subject and translate 'and from then on such words were not afraid of what might happen to them'.

12 This line has never been satisfactorily explained. There may be in *Hionios* some meaning which we cannot guess; or Catullus may be suggesting that the Ionian Sea is now as rough as Arrius's speech; or he may simply mean that after murdering the Latin language Arrius is now murdering the far more delicate and refined Greek—a ghastly crime in the eyes of a cultured Roman.

20

A specimen of Latin invective at its most gruesome. The victim was possibly P. Cominius, whose prosecution of C. Cornelius, an ex-tribune, made him highly unpopular.

1 **cana:** He was old enough to know better.

3 **bonorum:** Adjectives of doubtful gender should generally be taken as masculine in cases where there is no noun.

4–5 The periphrastic subjunctive for doubts about the future is not essential in prose and is too clumsy for verse, especially in the passive. **uocet:** Translate by a passive to preserve the order.

21

One of several attacks on Mamurra, who as an officer of Caesar piled up wealth, but by extravagance and debauchery dissipated it so completely that he became the *decoctor Formianus* of 40.5. *Mentula* is not a scansional substitute for *Mamurra* but a nickname equivalent to 'Lechery'. Mamurra's own name appears in two very scurrilous poems. See note on 13.1.

1 **Firmano saltu:** 'Thanks to his estate at Firmum.'

2 **qui:** 'for it . . .'. The antecedent is *saltu*.

3 **omne genus:** 'of every kind'; an unalterable phrase which can be attached to any case of a noun.

4 **exsuperat:** The subject is 'he'.

5 **concedo sit:** 'I allow him to be'. Fordyce translates the line 'I don't mind his being rich so long as he has no assets at all'. Note this meaning of *dum* (or *dum modo*, as in the next line) with subjunctive.

6 **modo ipse:** The hiatus makes some editors suspect the reading.

22

Catullus sends an invitation to Caecilius, who is otherwise unknown. The poem is addressed to the paper on which it is written—a bright idea which reappears in Horace and more than once in Ovid and Martial.

1 **tenero:** a word twice applied by Martial to Catullus himself. It was specially used of those who wrote about love.

2 **uelim dicas:** 'I want you to say'—a normal construction.

3 **ueniat:** 'that he must come'; a jussive subjunctive which even in prose can be used without *ut*. **Noui:** The word was not applied to Comum till 59 B.C., when the town was colonised by Caesar. The poem must have been written in or after that year.

NOTES

4 **moenia:** 'walled city', as regularly in Vergil. **Larium litus:** 'the Larian shore', i.e. the shore of the Larian lake (Lago di Como).

7 **uiam uorabit:** i.e. he will use all speed. Shakespeare uses the same words 'devour the way', and in Job we read that the warhorse 'swalloweth the ground'.

10 **roget morari:** Verbs of requesting and commanding (except *iubeo*) normally take a final clause.

12 **deperit:** transitive—'is dying for ...'. **impotente:** a dangerous word: consult the vocabulary. The ablative in *-e* is metrically convenient. Elsewhere Catullus has *elegante*. Other poets took the same liberty much more often.

13-14 **quo tempore, ex eo:** equivalent to *ex eo tempore quo*. **legit:** scan. **incohatam:** 'the beginning of his ...'. **Dindymi dominam:** the title of the poem, referring to the same person as *Magna Mater* in line 18, i.e. Cybele. **misellae:** 'the love-sick girl'. Cf. 58.21.

15 **medulla:** the seat of tender emotion. Cf. 58.16.

16-18 **Sapphica ... doctior:** 'lady more poetical than Sappho's muse', i.e. than the poetess Sappho. Catullus gives his approval to the special sense of *doctus* in which, even more than *tener*, it was later to be applied to himself.

est uenuste Caecilio incohata: 'Caecilius has made a charming beginning of ...'. The repetition of *incohata* (which implies 'unfinished') is a hint that it is time for Caecilius to tear himself away from the lady's tenacious embrace and get on with the job.

23

1-2 **hesterno die:** a common substitute for *heri*, as are *hodierno die* and *crastino die* for *hodie* and *cras*. **otiosi lusimus:** 'Having nothing to do we amused ourselves' (Fordyce). *ludo* was used of writing light verse, but in translating we must not anticipate line 4. **in meis tabellis:** 'with my wax tablets'. Verses scribbled on these could be easily erased; finished poems were written on papyrus. See line 2 of the previous poem. Evidently both poets wrote on the same tablets, which were passed backwards and forwards. See line 6.

3 **conuenerat esse delicatos:** 'We had agreed to be frivolous.' *delicatus* has so many meanings that it is impossible to be sure what Catullus means. Editors suggest 'to enjoy ourselves', 'to frolic', 'to be gentlemen of leisure', and 'to be naughty'. The last is perhaps correct, for the *noui poetae* had no objection to impropriety, so long as it was light-hearted.

4 **uersiculos:** not 'little' but 'playful' verses.

5 **numero:** 'measure' or 'metre'. **illoc:** an early form which did not survive.

6 **reddens ... uinum:** 'giving and taking as we joked and wined'.

7 **atque:** omit. **tuo ... facetiisque:** 'fired by your brilliance and humorous sallies'.

9 **iuuaret:** not 'helped' but 'gave pleasure to ...'.

11 **toto lecto:** 'all over my bed'. **indomitus:** 'uncontrollable'. **furore:** not 'fury' but, as often in Vergil, 'frenzy'.

13 **simul:** 'in your company'—a colloquialism.

14 **labore:** 'torment'.

16 **iucunde:** 'my dear fellow'. The word is regularly used of a friend who pleases.

17 **dolorem:** 'pain' or 'heart-ache'; 'grief' is too strong.

18 **caue:** For the scansion see note on 5.27. Evidence for the existence of a third conjugation form is very slight. **caue sis:** 'beware of being' or 'mind you are not'. **audax:** 'overbold'.

19 **ocelle:** 'apple of my eye'.

20 **reposcat:** 'exact'.

21 **uemens:** 'forceful' or 'imperious', (=*uehemens*). **caueto:** an emphatic form. We might translate 'offend her at your peril'.

24

For Scazons see Appendix II.

1 **Suffenus:** no doubt the poetaster's real name. It is met nowhere else. **probe:** 'well'—a common colloquialism.

3 **idemque:** perhaps 'but unfortunately'. **plurimos:** 'more than anyone'.

5 **sic ut fit:** 'in the usual way'. **palimpseston:** Though 'palimpsest' is a recognised English word, it has not quite the right meaning. Better 'paper used before'. Papyrus, like parchment, could be cleaned.

6 **relata:** 'set down'. **carta ... membranae:** 'royal sheets, brand-new rolls, brand-new knobs, red leather strings on the wrapper'. The strings were usually made of papyrus, which was cheaper. Most editors take *membranae* as nominative plural, but an epithet would surely be called for.

8 **derecta ... aequata:** 'everything ruled with lead and smoothed with pumice'. Lines to guide the writer were ruled with red lead, not the lead in a pencil, which of course had not been invented. For *pumice* see note on 1.2.

9 **legas:** *Cum* 'when' normally takes present indicative. The subjunctive is fairly common where a second person singular has the force of French *on*. The emphatic *tu* here seems as definite as it can be, and the poem is addressed to Varus. This however is only a poetic convention; the poem is in no sense a personal letter to an individual—look at the last two lines—and probably *tu* preceding *ille* is due to the Roman love of antithesis.

bellus et urbanus: 'fine city-bred gentleman' (Simpson).

10 **unus:** 'mere' or 'ordinary'—a Ciceronian usage.

11 **rursus:** perhaps 'by contrast'. **abhorret:** a difficult word, explained as either 'he is absurd' or 'he is inconsistent'. Perhaps we may paraphrase 'He changes so much that he is unrecognisable'. **mutat:** The active is used intransitively by Cicero and Livy, but the passive is more usual.

12 **putemus:** deliberative subjunctive. **modo:** The final vowel (variable in Lucretius and earlier poets but short elsewhere in Catullus) is probably lengthened before *sc-*. Catullus lengthens short vowels before *sp-*, *st-*, and *scr-*. **scurra:** 'wit', in later Latin 'buffoon'.

13 **scitius:** one of many emendations for the untranslatable *tristius* of the MSS—'cleverer'.

15 **simul:** equivalent to *simulatque*. **neque idem umquam est:** 'and yet he is never'.

17 **tam ... se:** 'he is so pleased with himself'.

18 **nimirum:** not 'no doubt' but 'of course'. **idem:** 'in the same way', an internal accusative with *fallimur*, which like the Greek middle voice means 'we deceive ourselves'. Cf. Vergil's *inutile ferrum cingitur* 'he girds on himself his useless sword' (where the accusative is external).

19 **Suffenum:** 'a Suffenus'.

20 **possis:** generic subjunctive (as in French) after a negative antecedent.

21 **manticae quod:** 'the part of the knapsack which ...'—a reference to a fable of Aesop. We carry our neighbour's vices before our eyes, our own behind our back.

25

A trifle, light as air, which brings out the poet's merry spirit, his devotion to his friend, and his detestation of long-winded and uninspired verse.

1 **plus oculis:** The use of an ablative of comparison with an adverb is frequent in verse but rare in prose.

2 **iucundissime:** See note on 23.16. **munere isto:** a bold ablative, equivalent to *propter munus istud*. What the *munus* was is made clear in line 5.

3 **odio Vatiniano:** 'As Vatinius hates you.' We had the reason in poem 6.

5 **cur:** 'that'; relative as in 5.11. **male perderes:** 'plague me to death'.

6 **isti clienti:** 'that client of yours', a real or imaginary person defended by Calvus in the courts and rewarding him with rubbish.

7 **impiorum:** Editors give 'sinners', 'outcasts', and 'uninspired knaves'. Perhaps 'blasphemous rogues', who pretend to be inspired by the *di*.

8 **quod si:** 'But if', as regularly in Cicero. **nouum et repertum:** 'novel, carefully chosen'.

9 **dat Sulla:** 'is a present to you from Sulla'. The tense is an idiom common in Vergil. Advocates were not paid, but could receive gifts or legacies. **litterator:** 'elementary teacher'—a term of contempt.

10 **non ... beate:** 'I am not grieved but more than delighted'.

12 **sacrum:** literally 'accursed'; perhaps 'damnable' would do. The exclamatory accusative is normal.

13 **scilicet:** meaning doubtful: 'of course', 'actually', 'of all men' have been suggested.

14–15 **misti:** See note on 9.7. **continuo:** probably an adverb 'then and there'. **die Saturnalibus, optimo dierum:** 'on the day of the Saturnalia, the best of days'. For the separation of *die optimo* by the appositive *Saturnalibus* cf. Vergil's *ignauum fucos pecus* and *dirum tineae genus*, both in *Georgic* iv. In Republican times the feast of Saturn occupied only one day, December 17th.

16 **non ... abibit:** 'No, no, you bad man; you won't get away with it like that.' *false*, the reading of the MSS, seems incapable of conveying the playful meaning required, and it is likely that Catullus wrote *salse*, 'you witty fellow'.

17 **si luxerit:** 'as soon as the sun is up'. *si* with the future perfect denoting not condition but time is found in both verse and prose. The closest parallel is Vergil's *si nona diem . . . Aurora extulerit* (*Aeneid* v 64–65). But Cicero uses the idiom more than once, e.g. *ad litteras ueniam si pauca ante dixero* (*Philippic* xiv 6).

18–19 **scrinia:** 'shelves' is more suitable than the literal meaning 'book-box'. **Caesios . . . Suffenum:** The two plurals (which should be retained unaltered) mean Caesius, Aquinus, and other writers of the same sort, a common idiom. The one singular should be noted—'Suffenus himself' or 'the one and only Suffenus'. **omnia uenena:** 'all the poisonous stuff'. This shows that *Caesios* etc. means 'the works of Caesius' etc., but we need not say this: we can say in English 'I will buy a Vergil'.

20 **suppliciis:** a very strong word—'drastic penalties'.

22 **illuc . . . attulistis:** 'to the place from which you dragged your miserable feet'. Notice the double meaning of *pedem*. *malus* is a much stronger word than 'bad'; cf. Horace's *malus fur* 'a thieving scoundrel'.

23 **saecli incommoda:** 'curses of our generation'. The plague of bad poets (who often insisted on reading their poems aloud to their unfortunate friends) lasted for several more generations.

26

The slow Scazons express the poet's complaint more effectively than tripping Hendecasyllables would have done.

1 **Sabine . . . Tiburs:** vocatives in agreement with *funde*, *seu* being equivalent to *uel*.

2–4 **autumant:** a solemn old-fashioned word for 'declare', 'insist'. **quibus non est cordi:** 'who have no wish'. **Tiburtem . . . Sabinum:** Tibur was more fashionable than the Sabine district.

5 **sed:** 'any-way'.

6 **fui libenter:** 'I was glad to be'. **suburbana:** not 'suburban' (which sounds scornful) but 'close to the City'.

7 **pectore exspui:** perhaps 'cleared my chest of'. **malam:** perhaps 'villainous'. See note on line 22 of the previous poem.

8 **uenter:** 'greediness'.

9 **dedit:** with *mihi meus uenter*.

10 **Sestianus:** 'of Sestius' (P. Sestius, quaestor when Cicero was consul).

13-20 **frequens:** 'incessant' or 'hacking'. **grauedo frigida ... frigus:** Preserve the echo in translating. Perhaps 'a heavy chill ... their chilliness'. The Romans, like ourselves, often described an oration as 'frigid', but we cannot apply this word to a cold.

15 **recuraui:** 'nursed myself back to health'. **urtica:** 'nettles'— a standard remedy for chills.

19 **recepso:** 'again take up' or 'give house-room to' (an old form of *recepero*).

21 **tunc cum:** 'only when'. **malum:** as in line 7.

27

Volusius evidently wrote his chronicles in verse.

1 **cacata carta:** 'filthy waste-paper' (Cornish). With the assonance cf. Vergil's *moriamur et in media arma ruamus*.

4 **si ... essem:** The lovers had had a minor dispute.

5 **iambos:** See note on 13.2.

6 **pessimi poetae:** Lesbia meant Catullus, but he pretends not to recognise this. **tardipedo deo:** Vulcan had been thrown out of heaven by his father Jupiter. Note the omission of *se*, as occasionally in Cicero and often in Caesar.

8 **infelicibus:** 'accursed', a ritual term applied to the wood used for burning up evil things.

9 **hoc:** Editors differ as to whether *hoc* is accusative and *pessima* feminine singular, or *hoc* ablative and *pessima* neuter plural.

10 **iocose lepide:** For the asyndeton (absence of *et*) cf. *amant amantur* in 58.20.

11 **creata ponto:** Venus was supposed to have been born from the sea.

12-15 Idalium, Amathus, and Golgi were haunts of Venus in Cyprus. Ancona (here called by its Greek name Ancon) was on the Italian coast of the Adriatic, Dyrrachium on the opposite coast. Cnidus was on the S.W. coast of Asia Minor. All these places were centres of Venus-worship. Urii is unknown.

apertos: probably 'exposed' or 'open to view'. **tabernam:** 'hostelry'.

16 **acceptum ... redditumque:** 'enter as received and paid'—a metaphor from book-keeping. Notice the old form *face*.

18 **interea:** a favourite word of Catullus. Cf. 25.21 and 31.7.

19 As the next line must be kept till last, translate 'you mass of rusticity and witlessness'.

28

1 **Pipleium ... montem:** i.e. to write poetry. Pipleia was a spring sacred to the muses.

2 **furcillis:** *furca* or *furcilla eicere, expellere, detrudere,* was a stock metaphor. *furcilla* seems to have no diminutive signification.

29

Cinna, like Catullus, was a keen follower of the Alexandrian School, and contemptuous of those who did not share his enthusiasm. Later Romans found his poem about Zmyrna (a woman, not a town) excessively obscure, the penalty of too much devotion to *doctrina*.

1–2 **Zmyrna:** So we say 'Hamlet' when we mean the play about Hamlet. Notice the Greek spelling. **nonam ... hiemem:** 'nine harvests and nine winters after it was begun has at last been published'. The mention of both summer and winter emphasises the immense pains lavished by Cinna on his very short work. *edita* is actually a participle, the main verb being either *mittetur* in line 5 or a word in the missing line.

3 **Hortensius:** generally identified as Q. Hortensius Hortalus, the *patronus* who failed to save Verres, and who seems to have been one of the *noui poetae*, though a generation older than most of them. He was a friend of Catullus, as we find in poem 32, but is here teased for producing too much verse in too little time. *uno* agrees with some word in the missing line, probably *anno* (or *mense* or even *die*), though *in pede stans* (used later by Horace of another hasty scribbler) has been brilliantly suggested. *milia* indicates a genitive plural such as *uersiculorum*, and we must supply some verb such as *edidit*.

5–6 Keep the name of the poem where Catullus has placed it. **penitus:** 'all the way'. **cauas undas:** 'deep waters'. **Satrachi:** a river in Cyprus which figures in the story of Zmyrna.

cana ... peruoluent: 'the greying generations will long continue to read'. *peruoluent* (four syllables—a liberty often taken by Lucretius) refers to the unrolling of a poem written on a roll. Cf. Juvenal's *diuina Philippica, uolueris a prima quae proxima*. Simpson's 'turn the pages' is anachronistic.

7–8 Catullus is much ruder to Volusius than to Hortensius. See poem 27.

Paduam: not the town (which was *Patauium*) but a branch of the Po (*Padus*). **ipsam:** 'their birthplace'. **laxas tunicas:**

'voluminous wraps'. **saepe:** 'again and again'—often a good translation. Both *laxas* and *saepe* implied that Volusius provided unlimited quantities of wastepaper for wrapping up the ancient equivalent of fish and chips.

30

We do not know the occasion of this little poem. Some think it is ironical; but more probably Cicero had got Catullus out of some scrape—*patronus* usually implies 'counsel for the defence'—and the poet's tribute is sincere. Cicero's clients, though as a rule acquitted, were in most cases probably guilty, and we may suspect that Catullus was no exception. Observe the extraordinary simplicity and naturalness of the wording.

1 **Romuli nepotum:** a dignified phrase, used partly because *Romanorum* cannot be fitted into Hendecasyllables, but chiefly to cover all Romans from the very beginning, and so lead up to the next two lines. Catullus' prophecy proved true.

5–7 Translate *poeta* and *patronus* as if they were genitive plural, and so preserve the order and emphasis of the Latin.

31

One of the best loved of Catullus' poems, conceived if not written when he visited his brother's tomb in the Troad, perhaps on his way to Bithynia. Its simplicity and sincerity are outstanding, but it is composed with the utmost skill and verbal felicity. Note the purposeful repetition of the gentle consonant *m*, and the perfection of the last line.

1 It is unfortunately impossible to keep *multas* first in a straightforward translation. Begin with *uectus*.

2 **aduenio:** 'I come'; the tense can be retained. **miseras:** 'poor', and so in line 6. **has ad inferias:** 'to make these offerings' (not 'rites', which will not do in line 8).

3 **donarem:** The sequence of tenses is due to the thought 'My intention in coming was to . . .'. **mortis:** possessive genitive; the gift belongs to, or is due to, death.

5–6 **quandoquidem:** Keep the heavy sound—'inasmuch as'. **mihi:** dative of person affected, used in Latin with verbs of taking away as well as with verbs of giving. Cf. French *voler à quelqu'un*. **indigne, adempte:** Scan both words.

7 interea: This favourite word is difficult here. Perhaps Catullus means that he is doing all that is possible in the circumstances. Translate 'as things are'.

8 tradita sunt: probably not 'have been handed down' but 'have been presented (by me)', or more neatly 'I have presented'. Catullus uses the verb elsewhere with this sense.

9 fraterno: Latin regularly employs adjectives for which a noun must be substituted in English. **multum:** adverbial with *manantia*; perhaps 'streaming' will cover both words.

10 aue atque uale: the regular farewell to the dead. In spite of certain translators it must of course be kept to the end. Cf. *Aeneid* xi 97–98 *salue aeternum . . . aeternumque uale*, which is much more self-consciously 'poetical'.

32

Grief at his brother's death prevents the poet from composing the original works promised to his friend Ortalus; instead he is sending some translations from Callimachus. These may or may not have included the poem which follows in the MSS (no. 64 in this selection). On the other hand we may safely identify Ortalus with the Hortensius pilloried in 29. Evidently the severe strictures of that poem did not impair the friendship between the two men. So too we shall find severe criticisms of Furius, one of the *comites* to whom in 51 Catullus entrusted a most intimate message.

1 confectum: Substitute a main clause followed by 'and'.

2 doctis uirginibus: 'the poetic maids', i.e. the muses.

3 potis: 'able'—indeclinable and interchangeable with *pote*, which is found also in Cicero and is used without *est*. **expromere:** exact meaning uncertain; perhaps 'set before you'.

4 mens animi: a phrase used by Lucretius also for active intelligence—'the imagination of my heart'. **tantis malis:** 'on such a sea of her own troubles is she tossed'.

5–6 Lethaeo gurgite manans: 'flowing from the swirling waters of Lethe' (a river of the underworld).

7 Rhoeteo: Rhoeteum was a promontory near Troy. Here the word is an adjective.

8 ereptum: with *ex oculis*. See note on line 1.

10–11 amabilior: Do not translate 'dearer', which would destroy the link with *amabo*.

12 tua morte: probably instrumental with *maesta* 'made sad'.

13 **concinit:** Note the intensive prefix, as in Caesar's favourite *conicio*.

14 **Daulias:** Procne, having killed her son to punish his father Tereus, king of Daulia in Phocis, was turned into a nightingale which everlastingly lamented the deed.

16 **expressa:** a standard word for 'translated'. For the principal parts see the vocabulary. **Battiadae:** See note on 10.2.

17 **uagus:** 'wandering'; like *uagor* a favourite word with Catullus.

18 **effluxisse:** 'slipped', a metaphor used by Cicero even without *animo*.

19 **missum:** probably 'thrown', a common meaning. **sponsi munere:** 'as her suitor's gift'; a rather bold use of the instrumental ablative. Cf. 31.8. *sponsus* should mean 'formally betrothed', but in *Epistles* I ii 28 Horace uses it in the same way, anticipating the betrothal, and in *Aeneid* iv 35 Vergil takes an even greater liberty by calling suitors *mariti*.

21–22 It is simplest to take *miserae oblitae* as possessive genitive with *ueste*, and *locatum* as nominative in agreement with *quod*; but *miserae oblitae* may be dative of disadvantage with *excutitur* (cf. *huic* in line 24) and *locatum* accusative after *oblitae*.

23 'And lo! there it rolls headlong in steep descent.' In *Georgic* i 203 Vergil imitates this line and uses *atque* to give the same sense of vividness and speed. *illud* has its deictic or fully demonstrative force: it is not a mere subject to *agitur*, which does not need one.

24 **huic:** demonstrative like *illud*, and contrasted with it. **tristi:** perhaps dative, probably ablative. We may translate the line 'over the maiden's sad visage steals a guilty blush'.

33

After his unprofitable year in Bithynia (Spring 57 to Spring 56 B.C.) Catullus is delighted to leave for home, and eager to be off; but the opportunity to see some of the places sung by the poets is too good to be lost, and he is going to choose his own route regardless of his friends. The poem is one of his liveliest.

1 **egelidos:** This word, which in a few passages (e.g. *Aeneid* viii 610) seems to mean 'extremely cold', more often means 'pleasantly warm'. Note the contrast in Ovid, *Amores II* xi 10—*gelidum Borean egelidumque Notum*, where Boreas is the north wind, Notus the south. Here we might translate it 'gentle', or 'balmy'.

3 **silescit aureis:** 'is silenced by the breezes'. Inscriptions suggest that in the time of Catullus, Caesar, and Cicero *i* in the first two declensions was written *ei* (monosyllabic). Remember that our MSS of these authors are medieval, and the spelling rarely departs, as it does here, from that in vogue at the time they were written.

4-5 **linquantur:** best translated by the active imperative. *linquo* without prefix is common in poetry and occasionally found in Cicero.

Phrygii campi: Phrygia and Bithynia overlapped; Nicaea was an important city of Bithynia. **aestuosae:** 'sultry'. Notice the many adjectives formed by adding *-osus* to the stem of a noun. In poem 1 we had *laboriosus*, and in all Catullus uses twenty-five.

6 **claras Asiae urbes:** Here as often *Asia* is the Roman province in western Asia Minor. The famous cities to be visited would certainly include Ephesus with its magnificent temple of Artemis, one of the seven wonders of the world; probably Sardis and Smyrna; possibly some of the islands off the coast.

7 **praetrepidans:** 'fluttering with anticipation'. Though in English 'trepidation' always denotes fear, *trepido* means to quiver with any emotion, e.g. hope or joy. The compound is found only here.

8 Take the words exactly as they come, relating *studio* to *laeti*. Be sure that you have kept *iam* in its place each time that it has occurred, and have translated it in the same way every time.

9 **o:** Never disregard this word, which in Latin, as Fordyce points out, always has an emotional content. Here 'You' or 'O you!' will perhaps do.

10 **simul:** not 'at the same time' but 'together'. See note on 23.13. Both idioms are Ciceronian.

11 **diuersae uarie:** The MSS read *diuerse uarie*. Most editors write *diuersae uariae*, but three successive words with the same ending are unlikely. In the Middle Ages *ae* was reduced to *e*, so that, as every carol-singer knows, *caeli* and *Mariae* became *celi* and *Marie*. What Catullus wrote is therefore a matter for speculation, and the reading of the Oxford text is the most satisfactory. *diuersae uiae* are 'scattered routes'; *uarie* perhaps means 'in differing ways': some *comites* may have made direct for the sea.

34

Love of home, an emotion peculiarly strong in English breasts, meant little to the Romans, with their fondness for owning numerous residences in town and country and for continually moving from one to another. The sentiments of this lovely poem have an immediate appeal for us, and its spontaneity and sincerity lift it far above the level of convention and artifice characteristic of so much Latin poetry.

1 The sound of this line cannot be reproduced in English. For the first substantive Tennyson suggested 'all-but-island'; but this is not a recognised term in English as *paene insula* is in Latin and *presqu'île* in French; so we must content ourselves with 'peninsula'. Grammarians should note that apart from *paene insula* the combination of adverb and noun is very much rarer in Latin than in English, though Fordyce quotes a number of examples. The only other one in Catullus will be found in line 10 of the next poem. Sirmio (Sirmione) is linked by an isthmus, which is sometimes submerged, to the southern shore of Benacus (Lago di Garda), through which flows the Mincius (Mincio).

2 **ocelle:** Like *oculus* this is a favourite Catullan word for something very precious. Here it is better to substitute 'gem' or 'jewel'. **liquentibus stagnis:** Look up both words in the vocabulary.

3 **uasto:** This word can mean either 'huge' or 'awesome' or both at once, as very often in the *Aeneid*. **uterque Neptunus:** 'either Neptune', i.e. Neptune as lord of salt water and fresh. The same adjective was applied by later poets to Diana and Phoebus, with reference to the dual capacity of these deities.

4 **libenter, laetus:** The co-ordination of adverb and adjective is found even in Cicero, but had better be modified in English.

5 **mi ipse credens:** 'believing my own eyes'. Note (1) that two constructions, *credo* with dative and *credo* with infinitive, are combined; (2) that there is no accusative with the infinitive. Catullus may be using a standard Greek construction of which we shall have an undoubted example in line 2 of the next poem; but he may be merely omitting *me* (which would be awkward after *mi*) as Caesar not infrequently omits *se* or *eum*.

Thuniam atque Bithunos: The Thynians and Bithynians were two Thracian tribes who settled in the district normally referred to by one name or the other, *Bithynia* being the prevailing form. If the MSS are correct, Catullus retains the Greek *u* here, though in other poems we find *y* in both names.

7 **o:** Cf. lines 12 and 13, and see note on line 9 of the preceding poem. If the word is retained here it must be spelt 'oh'. **solutis curis:** 'than release from care'. The participle has the force of a verbal noun, as in *ab urbe condita* 'from the foundation of the City', and in Horace's *ademptus Hector* 'the removal of Hector'.

9 **uenimus:** scan. **larem:** The *lares* were household gods, but the singular should be translated 'home' or 'hearth'.

10 The long words suggest the long absence and the slow, peaceful settling on the bed. *desidero* is not a synonym for *cupio*: it denotes a yearning for someone or something loved in the past.

11 'This it is that by itself atones for toils so great' or 'all our toils'.

12 **salue:** Avoid 'hail'. Perhaps 'greeting' or 'good day to you' would do, and 'my' would give the force of *o*. Omit *atque*, which serves only to link the two imperatives, and be careful with *ero*.

13 **gaudente, uosque:** The MSS read *gaudete uos quoque*, which does not scan. The accepted emendation *uosque* gives the same sense; but *-que* for *quoque* is rarely if ever found (see note on 2.3), and if *uosque* means 'and you' the postponement till after *gaudete* is unique in Catullus, though often paralleled in Ovid two generations later. If Bergk's emendation *gaudente* is accepted, we get, not 'rejoice in your master: rejoice you also', but 'rejoice when' or 'since your master rejoices; and you . . . laugh'.

Lydiae: The MSS read *lidie* (see note on line 11 of the previous poem), which is meaningless. *limpidae*, *liquidae*, and many other substitutes have been suggested, but the old emendation in our text is almost certainly right. Benacus was in Etruscan territory, and it was universally believed that the Etruscans were immigrants from Lydia. So Vergil in *Aeneid* ii calls Tiber Lydian. In translating remember that *lacus* is masculine.

35

The owner of a superannuated yacht tells his guests all about it. The owner is generally assumed to be Catullus, who does not elsewhere make himself the mouthpiece of an unnamed or imaginary person. The metre is the pure Iambic Trimeter, no spondees, tribrachs, or anapaests being admitted. The only other poems in this extremely difficult metre are XXIX (a scurrilous attack on Caesar and Pompey, not included in this selection) and the parody of the present poem found among the juvenile works attributed to Vergil.

1 **phaselus:** a Greek word for 'bean'. Here as in *Georgic* iv it means a bean-shaped boat; surely not a proper name, as in James Elroy Flecker's translation. **phaselus ille:** not 'that pinnace' but 'the pinnace yonder'. Though the noun is masculine the boat should be called 'she' by English convention.

2 **fuisse celerrimus:** a Greek construction; observe the case of the adjective, and see note on line 5 of the previous poem. Catullus has given the line all possible lightness. For the gender of the adjective, which logically should follow that of *nauium*, cf. Cicero's *Indus fluminum maximus* and Horace's *optime rerum* 'you best of creatures'.

3 **impetum:** 'speed'. **trabis:** 'timber'.

6–13 Notice that the poet traces the vessel's course backwards to its starting-point, and consult the map.

6 **opus:** 'need', or substitute 'necessary'.

8 **nobilem:** 'renowned' for its natural beauty, its scholars and sailors, and of course the Colossus.

9 **Propontida:** final vowel lengthened before two consonants in the next word. So Vergil writes *tribolaque traheaeque* and *fontesque fluuiique*. See also note on 66.357. Propontis is marked on the map; what is its modern name?

10 **post phaselus:** See note on line 1 of the previous poem, and cf. Vergil's *late regem* and Cicero's *publice testem*. Translate 'pinnace-to-be'.

13 **Amastri:** Greek vocative.

14 **tibi:** The port and ridge are treated as one, like the twins in line 26.

17 **imbuisse:** 'first dipped'.

18 **impotentia:** See notes on 22.12 and (for the scansion) line 9 above.

19 Understand *siue* before *laeua*.

21 **secundus:** 'astern', *Iuppiter* here standing for the wind sent from heaven. **simul:** with *incidisset*. **pedem:** Consult the vocabulary.

22–23 **deis sibi:** 'to the gods for her'.

24 **nouissimo:** 'the last', i.e. the Adriatic. **lacum:** Benacus, if the pinnace belonged to Catullus.

25 **prius fuere:** 'belong to the past'.

27 **gemelle Castoris:** best translated 'Castor's twin', i.e. Pollux.

36

A translation, modified to suit the subject of Catullus' relations with Lesbia, of an ode by the Lesbian poetess Sappho. Catullus has been criticised for omitting some of Sappho's words and inserting words of his own; but this is inevitable, especially when a translator retains such a difficult metre as the Sapphic. Milton took far greater liberties in his metrical versions of psalms, where insertions abound. The poem is clearly complete without the fourth quatrain tacked on to it in the MSS.

2 **si fas est**: 'if it is lawful to say it'.

5 **dulce ridentem**: borrowed by Horace, *Odes I* xxii. *dulce*, an internal object, may be translated by an adverb. Cf. *suaue olentis* in 62.7 and *dulce rideat* in 62.184. **simul**: for *simul ac*, as often in Latin—'as soon as'.

7 **nihil est super**: 'nothing is left' ($=superest$). The missing line *may* have been *uocis in ore*, but several other guesses have been made.

9 **tenuis**: 'subtle'. **sub artus**: 'into the depths of my frame'. Vergil frequently uses *sub* in this way.

10 **suopte**: an old emphatic form of *suo*.

11 **gemina**: Scansion shows that this word agrees with *nocte*, not with *lumina*—an astonishing case of the transfer of an epithet (hypallage). But Catullus may have written *geminae*, to agree with *aures* as in 65.75.

37

The principle 'You may be dead tomorrow, so have a good time now' had already appeared in Greek poetry, and later Tibullus and Propertius were to follow Catullus closely in likening the opportunity for love to a short-lived day. In the form 'Life is short, so come and have a drink' the theme was to be worked to death by Horace. Catullus handles this and all other such commonplaces with an absence of solemnity unique in Latin.

2 'the tattle of stodgy (or 'censorious') old men'.

3 **unius assis**: The *as* may have been worth about 5d. in purchasing power, but we can safely translate by 'at a single penny'.

5 Note the effectiveness of the rare monosyllabic ending, and cf. line 7 of the next poem. The *est* which follows there three lines later is dissimilar, being made by elision into a syllable of the previous word, like *malest* in 38.1.

6 **perpetua**: not 'perpetual' but 'unbroken', as in Caesar's *perpetua palus*.

7 **basia**: a colloquial word which Catullus seems to have been the first poet to employ. The same is true of *basiare* and *basiatio* in the next poem. The French and Italian derivatives, *le baiser* and *il bacio*, are no doubt familiar.

8 **usque altera:** probably 'yet another'; but some editors take *usque* to mean 'uninterruptedly'.

10 **fecerimus:** Scan the word, and compare with your grammar book. Translate 'we have made up'.

11 **conturbabimus illa:** a technical expression—'we will confuse the reckoning' or 'wreck the accounts', like a fraudulent bankrupt. **ne sciamus:** It was unlucky to count one's blessings.

12 **aut ... malus:** best translated 'and that no malicious person ...'. **inuidere:** not 'envy them' but 'cast an evil eye on them'.

13 **sciat:** Note the mood, and do not translate *cum* as 'when'.

38

This poem is similar in theme to its predecessor, the difference being that this time it is Catullus who does the kissing. Why did he, on this one occasion, write two poems so alike? Because, as he admits in line 10, he is *uesanus* and cannot help himself. Perhaps also, as the first word suggests, his mistress had commanded him to write the second.

1–2 **basiationes tuae:** The adjective is equivalent to an objective genitive *tui* (pronoun). The usual translation is 'kissings of you', which is intolerable English. Fordyce suggests 'kisses on your lips'; we might say 'kisses given to *you*'. Notice the extremely emphatic position of *tuae*. which editors seem to have missed, and which may give a clue to the exact form of Lesbia's command. **satis superque:** a standard expression—'enough and more than enough'.

3 'As great a number as that of the Libyan sand which ...' or more simply 'as many as the grains of Libyan sand that ...'. Note that though in examination compositions it is prudent to write *tantus, quantus, tot,* and *quot,* Cicero himself frequently wrote *tam magnus, quam multi* etc., as Catullus does here and in lines 7 and 9.

4 **lasarpiciferis:** 'silphium-bearing'. Silphium is the plant from which the Romans extracted asafoetida, a foul-tasting resin used in medicine.

Cyrenis: The plural form *Cyrenae* denotes what St. Luke in *Acts* ii calls 'the parts of Libya about Cyrene', i.e. the district called by the later Romans and by ourselves Cyrenaica. Cyrene was an important Greek colony founded by Battus, of whom we read in the next two lines.

5 **inter**: to be taken first. So Vergil more than once puts *circum* after its noun. **aestuosi**: See note on 33.5. The agreement of this adjective with *Iouis* is another daring hypallage; cf. 36.11. It was at this temple in the Siwa Oasis that Alexander was told that Zeus, not Philip, was his father.

6 **ueteris**: Cyrene was founded six centuries before Lesbia's time.

9 'To kiss you with so many kisses. . . .' We cannot in English 'kiss a person many kisses' (internal object) as Catullus could in Latin.

11 **curiosi**: defined by Plautus in his play *Stichus* as people *alienas res qui curant*, i.e. busybodies.

12 **possint**: possibly consecutive or final, but probably potential —'would be able to' or more simply 'could'. **mala**: Scan this word, and translate 'evil' or, as in the corresponding line of the previous poem, 'malicious'.

39

In this and the following poem, similar in theme but very different in tone, Catullus again shows his fondness for contrasting those he admires with those he does not. In the first he compares a woman of beautiful parts, but not lovely as a whole or endowed with subtle graces, with Lesbia who 'has the lot'; in the second he pours furious abuse on an entirely unattractive woman whom his contemporaries were crazy enough to compare with his own mistress.

1-2 **formosa**: As *forma* means 'shape' or 'lovely shape', *formosus* must mean 'shapely' or 'lovely as a whole', whereas *pulcer* may be applied to a pretty face, a well turned ankle, or the like. Having brought this out in the first couplet, Catullus gives the word another connotation in the second, and combines them both in the third. **multis**: 'in the eyes of many'. **candida . . . recta**: 'fair, tall, and straight'. **sic**: 'readily'.

3 A most difficult sentence to translate, especially as it must be related to *pulcerrima tota est* in line 5. Cornish translates 'But I demur to "beautiful" . . . she possesses all the beauties'; Whigham has 'But such things do not constitute beauty . . . Lesbia is . . . of particular beauty'. Both these versions disregard not only *totum . . . tota* but also the change from *formosa* to *pulcerrima*. Perhaps 'That all-embracing "lovely" I deny . . . her beauty is matchless and all-embracing' ('matchless' representing the superlative). Observe that *formosa*, meaning the word itself, is not declined: cf. Ovid, *Metamorphoses* xv 96, *aetas cui fecimus aurea nomen*.

4 **tam magno corpore:** See note on line 3 of the previous poem. Be careful not to make the phrase seem uncomplimentary: *corpus* can often be translated 'person'.

6 Keep *Veneres* to the end—'in her one self she has robbed all others of all the graces'.

40

1–4 A clear account of what the Romans admired in a woman.
nec minimo naso: 'with neither the smallest of noses'. **puella:** Her name, given in another poem, was Ameana. **nigris:** not to be translated 'black'! **ore sicco:** not 'dry mouth', which would give a wrong impression, but 'dry lips'. Lips were made for kissing. **sane:** 'to be frank'.

5 'mistress of the bankrupt of Formiae'. See the introductory note to poem 21.

6–7 **ten(=tene):** This and similar shortened forms are colloquialisms admitted even by Vergil. *ten* and *tecum* are emphatic —'Is it you that . . .? Is it with you that . . .?' **prouincia:** Catullus' home district, Cisalpine Gaul, remained a province till it was enfranchised five years after his death.

8 Keep the order—'What a generation of fools and nitwits!'

41

A poem to which the MSS have attached three lines (omitted here) from another poem.

1 **passer:** a common pet in Italy. Perhaps not a sparrow but a thrush or linnet: it is not even certain that the word denotes a particular species. **deliciae:** a regular word for 'pet', whether animal or human being. **puellae:** On no account translate 'girl'.

2 **quicum:** an early form used by Vergil and regularly by Cicero.

3 **primum digitum:** 'finger-tip'. Cf. the familiar *primum agmen*.

5 **desiderio:** 'heart's desire', an abstract noun often used of persons.

6 **carum nescio quid:** 'some sweet frolic'. When *nescio quis* is not followed by the subjunctive of an indirect question it means 'someone', not 'I don't know who'.

8 The reading is doubtful.

9 **possem:** a wish. **ipsa:** 'your missis', a domestic colloquialism used again in the next poem.

42

The best known of all the poems. It has often been imitated; but no imitation, from Ovid's elegy on a dead parrot to Skelton's *Lament for Philip Sparrow*, has the charm, compactness, or perfection of the original.

1 **O Veneres Cupidinesque:** See note on 4.12.

2 **quantum est:** 'all there are'. Catullus often uses the partitive genitive in this way. **uenustiorum:** perhaps 'of gracious spirit'—a reminiscence of *Veneres* which is difficult to bring out. As usual, the comparative need not be pressed.

4 A deliberative repetition of 41.1.

5 **plus oculis:** See note on 25.1.

7 **ipsam:** as in 41.9. **puella:** either 'a girl' or 'my lady'.

11–12 The impossibility of returning from the grave is a commonplace found in many writers before and after Catullus. But whereas Horace and Vergil propound it with all solemnity, Catullus does so with a smile. Hamlet's 'undiscovered country from whose bourn no traveller returns' is clearly reminiscent of this passage. We have already met a similar idea expressed with equal lightheartedness in poem 37.

13 Translate *male* and *malae* similarly, e.g. 'evil be to you, evil shades', or 'a curse on you, accursed shades'.

14 **Orci:** a common name for the underworld. **bella:** Be careful!

16 **male! o:** Observe the hiatus (absence of elision) where the poet pauses.

43

1–2 **iucundum:** This word cannot be taken until all except *inter nos perpetuumque* has been translated. **proponis:** indistinguishable in meaning from *promittere* in line 3. We might translate 'you give your word'.

5 **tota uita:** The ablative with *totus* is used for extent, both of time and space; e.g. *tota nocte* (Caesar), *tota Asia* and *urbe tota* (Cicero).

6 **sanctae amicitiae:** 'pledge of hallowed affection'. See note on 7.3–4, where, as here, Catullus is speaking of the passionate attachment between a man and a woman. It is sad that he was too *uesanus* to apply these words to the relationship between Lesbia and her husband, a relationship which he himself had treated with such contempt.

44

The shape of this little poem is borrowed from an epigram of Callimachus, but Catullus gives a poignant personal twist to the commonplace that lovers' promises—especially those of women—are made to be broken. Cf. Vergil's *uarium et mutabile semper femina* (*Aeneid* iv 569) and Verdi's '*La donna e mobile*' (*Rigoletto*).

1 **NVLLI**: an occasional substitute for *nemini*, as *nullo* is the regular substitute for *nemine*. **mulier**: The word is purposely chosen to anticipate the sweeping statement in the second couplet. Avoid words already used to translate *puella*, *domina*, and *amica*, and on no account write 'my woman'. Cornish well suggests 'the woman I love'.

Observe the emphatic position of *NVLLI*, and retain the order by the often useful device of making the main verb (*dicit*) parenthetical and treating the infinitive (*malle*) as the main verb—'No one, says ..., would she rather marry than me'. N.B. 'Prefer ... than' is not English.

2 **petat**: 'were to woo her'.

45

Catullus has made the psychological discovery that abuse of a person can be consistent with a passionate attachment to that person.

1 **mi ... male**: 'is always speaking ill of me'. Observe that *male dico*, like *bene dico*, takes the dative of the person spoken *about*; Lesbia is not abusing him to his face.

2 **de me**: Notice the strong emphasis, and cf. 38.2: he is the chief subject of her conversation. There is a similar emphasis on *assidue* two lines below. **disperam**: a wish. The compound verb means to perish utterly.

3 **sunt ... mea**: 'it's just the same with me'—a colloquialism. **deprecor**: Surprisingly this verb can mean to plead with, to plead for, or to plead against. The third meaning is required here—'I cry out against her'.

46

An extension of the same discovery—love can coexist with actual dislike.

2 **tenere**: 'to possess' or perhaps 'to make captive'.

3 **tantum:** 'merely'—a common meaning. **uulgus:** 'the mass of men'.

4 A strange equation of Catullus' illicit passion with the pure love of a father; but remember that almost every emotion of this unique poet was tinged with a strange tenderness.

5 **te cognoui:** Distinguish from *nouisse* in line 1—'I have found you out'.
impensius: 'more fiercely'. The word *impendo* means 'weigh out' or 'expend', but the participle has become an adjective meaning 'great' or 'strong'.

6 **mi:** 'in my eyes'. Cf. 39.1 *multis*. **uilior et leuior:** 'cheaper and more worthless'.

7 **qui potis est:** See notes on 10.3 and 32.3.

8 **magis, minus:** Preserve the antithesis, which is emphasised by the unusual position of these adverbs—'to feel love more, but goodwill less'.

47

Catullus disclaims all responsibility for the breach with Lesbia. Observe the purposeful repetition *me, mea, mea*, and the double emphasis on *nulla*: the poet believes that the devotion and faithfulness which he has shown have never been equalled.

1-2 **amatam [esse], amata est:** Translate the tense carefully. **uere:** with *dicere*—'with truth'.

3 **ullo foedere:** ablative; but we may render 'to any bond'.

4 **amore tuo:** Do not fail to look back at the note on 38.2. **ex parte mea:** 'on my side'.

48

Catullus returns to the theme of 46; but this time the emphasis is not on the dislike which he now feels in spite of his love, but on the love which persists unabated in spite of the dislike.

1 **HVC ... deducta:** Preserve the order—'To such a point has my mind been reduced'. **mea:** usually taken with *Lesbia*; but it is needed with *mens*, and given the punctuation printed in our text we must dismiss the other interpretation.

2 **ita:** Keep this word in its place—'so utterly'. **officio suo:** 'its own devotion'. The adjective is in an emphatic position and strengthened by *ipsa*, which need not be translated.

3 **optima:** 'the best of women'.

4 **omnia si facias:** 'whatever you might do'.

49

We have seen how distressed Catullus was by any unfaithfulness in a friend: here with surprising restraint he upbraids the friend who has robbed him of everything that made life worth living. Rufus is probably M. Caelius Rufus, whom we know to have been a paramour of Clodia, and to have broken with her two years before the death of Catullus.

1 **mihi:** dative of the agent, frequent in poetry. **frustra ac nequiquam:** synonyms, the weightier placed second as often in oratory—'in vain and to no purpose'. **credite amice:** 'believed to be a friend'. We do not expect a verb which governs the dative to be used personally in the passive; but Ovid has *uix credar*, and the personal passive, with a complement as here, is found in good prose.

2 **malo:** possibly a second adjective with *pretio*, but more probably a second noun with *magno*—'at a great price and to my grievous hurt', or, as Fordyce suggests, 'to my great cost and sorrow'.

3 **sicine ... mi:** 'is it thus you have stolen within me?' We have had similar contracted perfects before. **intestina:** not 'intestines' but 'vitals'.

4 **ei:** a monosyllabic interjection, here and in 66.92 used to emphasise *misero*—'oh how'.

6 **pestis:** 'bane', 'blight', 'ruin'—a noun which Cicero loved to apply to his enemies. The MSS read *pectus*, which seems impossible, though Simpson bravely extracts the meaning, 'the breast my friendship leaned upon'. **nostrae amicitiae:** 'of my love'. See note on 7.3-4.

50

Our poet was not the man to take things calmly: he swung rapidly from one extreme to the other. Overjoyed now at the vain hope that Lesbia and he were reconciled, he will soon plunge into black despair.

1-2 Translate freely, following the poet's order closely—'If something desired and longed for has ever been vouchsafed to one who is without hope, this is a delight to the heart in very truth'. **quicquam**: an early correction for the *quicquid* of the MSS, which is meaningless. Most editors accept Ribbeck's *si quoi* (or *cui*) *quid*, but we have had *si quicquam* as the first two words of 2 and 7.

3 Disregard the obeli: the line makes perfect sense if the last two words are enclosed between commas—'This therefore is a delight to me also, more precious than gold, that . . .'.

4-5 **cupido, insperanti**: Try to keep to the same translation of these words throughout. **ipsa:** 'of your own accord' or 'freely'.

6 **lucem . . . nota:** See note on 61.148. *lucem* means 'day'.

7-8 The last sentence yields no satisfactory sense, and many emendations have been suggested. Perhaps the simplest is to change *est optandus* to *rem optandam*—'Who can name anything more desirable than this life?'

51

One of Catullus' last poems, since the references to Caesar preclude a date of composition earlier than 55 B.C., when the poet had perhaps less than a year to live. Its verbal felicity, rich colours, and burning passion, together with the tremendous impact of the prolonged vocative (lines 1-14), leading up to a curt, grim main clause of seven simple words (lines 15-16), expanded into the excoriating fifth stanza, followed by another of unsurpassable sweetness—all these things combine to make it one of the most marvellous lyrics ever written. The metre is the Sapphic, perhaps chosen as a painful reminder of the very different poem (36) he had addressed to Lesbia in happier days. It was later to be used by Horace in an ode (II vi), of which the first stanza, beginning *Septimi, Gades aditure mecum*, is an unmistakable imitation of the present poem.

1 Furius and Aurelius had been roundly abused in earlier poems, but we have seen in other cases (e.g. that of Hortensius) that Catullus could abuse a man on one day and compliment him on another; and he himself has warned us in poem 46 that evil-speaking was compatible even with passionate love. Furius may have been the poet Furius Bibaculus. Of Aurelius nothing is known.

comites: Compare the line of Horace quoted above and supply *futuri*—'ready to be companions'.

2 **penetrabit:** Use an English present for this verb and for *gradietur* below. The future reference has already been made clear.

3 **ut:** 'where'—a very rare meaning which we shall meet again in poem 59. **Eoa:** 'eastern'—from the Greek word for 'dawn'. The same idea lies behind the word 'oriental'.

5 The Hyrcanians lived south of the Caspian. The Arabs were always considered by the Romans to be *teneri* or *molles* ('effeminate'). *Arabas* is a Greek third declension accusative. So Caesar writes *Allobrogas*.

6 The Sagae were Scythian nomads: the Parthian bowmen defeated Caesar's political ally M. Crassus three months after the first invasion of Britain.

7–8 **septemgeminus:** 'sevenfold'. This word, perhaps invented by Catullus, was later applied by Vergil also to the Nile and by Statius to Rome, the reference being to the seven mouths and seven hills respectively. **aequora:** 'plains', as sometimes in Vergil. Take this word out of the relative clause and make it the antecedent to *quae*.

9 **gradietur:** 'tramps' or 'trudges'.

10 **magni:** an obvious sincere compliment, despite the abuse previously heaped on the great man in poems 14 and 15.

11–12 **horribile aequor:** Haupt's not very convincing emendation of *horribilesque*, which gives good sense but is suspect because of the unparalleled hiatus. *aequor*, if correct, refers to the English Channel, which Catullus may have believed to be very stormy, though Caesar was later to report that it was smoother than the Mediterranean. For the division of *ultimos* between two lines cf. Horace's much more startling *u-xorius amnis*, which is also at the end of a Sapphic stanza. The comma after *Britannos* should be replaced by a dash in English.

13–14 The appropriate order can be effectively retained by keeping *temptare . . . parati* where it is and translating it by a main clause 'you are ready to face with me', followed by a colon. For *simul* see note on 33.10, and distinguish from the temporal meaning in line 18.

15–16 **pauca:** not an adjective with *dicta* but a noun—'a brief message'. **non bona dicta:** 'couched in no pleasant terms' (Simpson). *dicta* is a noun in apposition to *pauca*; it would hardly be possible *nuntiare dicta*.

17 **cum . . . ualeatque:** 'Bid her live and be happy' (Cornish).

18 'of whom she holds in her embrace three hundred at once'.

19 **identidem:** Where did we meet this word before?

20 Soften the harshness in translating—'exhausting the strength . . .'.

21 **nec respectet:** 'and let her not look to find . . .' (Cornish).

22-23 **prati . . . flos:** 'a flower on the edge of a meadow'—just as the Britons (line 12) were on the edge of the world. Note the elision at the end of the line. This beautiful simile was adapted by Vergil in *Aeneid* ix 435.

52

The final phase of the discovery announced in poems 45 and 46. The heart-broken lover now knows that it is possible to feel both love and hatred for the same person at the same time. Observe the perfect simplicity and naturalness of the language, the absence of one unnecessary word, and the devastating effect of the climactic ending. This tiny poem was the chief inspiration of Carl Orff's remarkable opera *Catulli Carmina*. Munro and Simpson quote the admirable comment of Fénelon—*Combien Ovide et Martiale, avec leurs traits ingénieux et façonnés, sont-ils au dessous de ces paroles négligées, ou le coeur saisi parle seul dans une espèce de désespoir!*

53

Catullus at last admits that reconciliation is impossible, and says goodbye without rancour to the mistress who even now occupies all his thoughts. The Choliambic metre ideally expresses the combination of despair and firm resolve.

1-2 **desinas, ducas:** The present subjunctive, which in prose is used for a command addressed to no particular individual (like the French infinitive in *agiter la bouteille*), in verse can be substituted for the imperative with no change of meaning. Note that in lines 9, 10, 11, and 19 of the present poem the imperative is used. The subjunctive is milder than the imperative, and Catullus purposely starts on a gentle note and ends with a peremptory command. The deliberate juxtaposition of *perisse* and *perditum*, which were treated as parts of the same verb, should be retained—'you must cease to be foolish; and what you see is lost, lost you must reckon'.

3 **candidi:** part of the predicate, to be translated after the verb.

4-5 **uentitabas:** indicative after temporal *cum*; occasionally found in Cicero, but not to be risked in an examination composition. **nobis:** The sudden change from second person to first is similar to that in *Propertius II* viii 18-19—*interitu gaudeat illa tuo. exagitet nostros manes* (quoted by Fordyce). **nulla:** Note the heavy emphasis: we cannot keep the word till last, but we might insert 'ever'.

6–7 A difficult sentence to translate. *ibi* has a temporal meaning, as often in Livy. Perhaps 'Then, when there was all that happy sport which you desired nor did your lady not desire'.

9 **nunc iam:** not a tautology; *iam non* or *non iam* is the normal Latin for 'no longer'. **impotens:** 'passion's slave' (Macmillan).

10 **quae:** Since 'her who' is ugly, translate 'one who'.

13 **requiret:** not 'require' but 'seek'.

14 **nulla:** in agreement with *tu*, but serving as an emphatic (colloquial) negative—'never once'.

15 **scelesta:** not 'villainous' as in Cicero, but 'unfortunate' as often in Plautus. Catullus speaks tenderly, not abusively. **uae te:** an emendation for the untranslatable *ne te*. *uae* usually takes the dative, as in Livy's famous *uae uictis*, but Plautus had already written *uae te*. Unless you are using old English throughout, do not accept the usual suggestion 'woe is thee'. Perhaps 'Unhappy woman, what a fate is yours!'

16 **cui . . . bella:** 'Who will think you fair?'

19 **destinatus obdura:** 'be resolute, stand firm'.

54

Dwelling now, not on the memory of past joys but on the cruel wounds inflicted on him, though as the most faithful of men he had done nothing to deserve them, the forsaken lover sinks into utter despair.

1–2 'If in recalling his kindnesses of other days a man can find any pleasure when he reflects that he is faithful. . . .'

3 **sanctam fidem:** 'his pledged word'. **nec foedere nullo:** 'nor in any compact . . .'. The double negative is inadmissible in English.

4 **numine:** 'sanctity' or 'majesty'.

5 Catullus was evidently unaware of the nearness of his death.

6 **ingrato:** 'thankless'.

7–8 'For whatever kindness men can show to anyone in either word or deed, all this in both word and deed has been shown by you.'

10 **excrucies:** Be careful with the deliberative subjunctive.

11 'Why do you not make a firm resolve, and both pull yourself back from where you are. . . .'

13 **longum amorem:** 'a long-felt passion'.

14 **hoc ... efficias:** 'this, by whatever means you can, you must accomplish'. For the subjunctive see note on line 1 of the previous poem.

15 **hoc ... peruincendum:** 'this you must carry through to victory'. The spondaic ending, rare in elegiacs, suggests a prolonged effort.

16 **siue ... siue non pote:** Reverse the order—'be it possible or impossible'. Catullus defies dull logic, as does Vergil in describing the efforts of the oarsmen in *Aeneid* v—*possunt quia posse uidentur*.

18 **extremam:** 'at the last'.

19 **puriter:** an archaic form used in a prayer, as often in all languages. Not 'purely', which would give a wrong impression, but 'blamelessly'. Catullus is thinking as usual of loyalty to pledged faith.

21 **quae:** The MSS read *seu*, for which *heu* has also been suggested. **torpor:** literally 'numbness'; perhaps 'palsy'.

22 **ex omni pectore:** In 61.25 we shall have *tota de mente*, and similar expressions were used by Tibullus and Ovid. We might paraphrase 'entirely from my breast', but a literal translation of the Latin idiom is possible in English.

23 **contra:** an adverb—'in return'.

24 **quod:** relative of course (= *id quod*); translate the clause 'a thing which is impossible', changing the commas to dashes or brackets without disturbing the order.

25 **ipse ... opto:** 'I pray that I may myself be healed'.

26 **pietate:** The translation should accord with that of *pium* in line 2.

55

This little poem presents us with two problems.

(1) In line 1 shall we read *uestra* or *nostra*, which has equal MS authority? The words could easily be confused, since Catullus may, like Plautus, have written *uostra*, and in uncial writing *NOSTRA* and *VOSTRA* look very much alike. There is the same problem in Plautus, *Mostellaria* iii 2, where the MSS are divided between *noster senex* and *uoster senex*. Here most editors read *nostra*, and suggest that, as in poem 4, Catullus is bewailing his own poverty; but elsewhere he berates Furius savagely for his debts and penury; and there is another strong reason for rejecting *nostra*, namely that in no other poem does he profess to address an

acquaintance and then talk about nobody but himself. *uestra* for *tua* presents no difficulty, as we have met this liberty already in 18.20 and shall meet it again in 61.151. Here the word may mean 'belonging to your family'.

(2) In line 2 how shall we render *opposita*, which is used with two meanings as a joke? This cannot be sacrificed without making the poem pointless. The meanings are 'facing' and 'mortgaged', and there is no English word capable of conveying both.

1–4 **Austri, etc:** Either retain the four names Auster, Favonius, Boreas, and Apheliotes, or, as three of these are unfamiliar to English readers, substitute South, West, North, and East in that order.

milia . . . ducentos: understand 'sesterces'. By Lewis and Short's reckoning (one sesterce = 2½d.) this would amount only to £140. If we allow for the decline in purchasing power since these scholars wrote, we get perhaps £650—a tiny mortgage indeed. Possible renderings of these four lines are:

(1) 'Furius, your little place in the country is not shaken by the blasts of the South, nor those of the West, the cruel North, or the East. But the 15,200 sesterces borrowed on it—*they* shake it!'

(2) 'Furius, your little place in the country does not feel any draught from the south, or from the west, the cruel north, or the east. But the £650 mortgage—it feels *that* draught!'

Now try to base a translation on 'secure' or 'security'.

56

Unlike Horace, Catullus does not continually sing the praises of wine. Perhaps, as in the case of Julius Caesar, his self-indulgence did not include a fondness for food and drink. This may be merely a playful imitation of Homer and other Greek poets who called for stronger drink, unlike Anacreon, who in two poems put water first and ordered his 'boy' to bring plenty of it!

1 'Boy, server of the good old Falernian.' *uetulum* is the regular epithet of this very choice wine.

2 **inger:** 'fill up'. Notice the very rare shortened imperative, and cf. the normal *dic, duc, fac*, and *fer*.

amariores: Seneca in letter 63.5 remarks that in old wine the *amaritudo* is a source of special pleasure. Fordyce, quoting this passage, suggests 'of a dryer vintage', but himself prefers 'mixed with less water'. But there seems to be no other passage where the word has this meaning, and here it would be a weak anticipation of the last three lines. Moreover Horace in *Odes III* xiii describes *merum* (neat wine) as *dulce*, and it would be strange if Catullus used *amarum*, the regular opposite of *dulce*, to stress the neatness of *merus Thyonianus*.

3 **magistrae**: 'mistress of the revels' (Cornish). It was usual to choose a *magister* or *arbiter bibendi*, who decided in what proportions the wine and water were to be mixed. There seems to be no other mention of a female counterpart. The identity of Postumia is unknown.

4 'tipsier than the tipsy grape' (literally 'berry').

6-7 **ad . . . migrate**: 'make your home with kill-joys'. Cf. 38.2. **merus Thyonianus**: 'neat', 'pure', or 'unspoilt Thyonian', i.e. wine of Bacchus, who is called Thyoneus by Horace and Ovid. With the adjective we must supply either *deus* (just as wine is often called *Bacchus*) or possibly the Greek word for wine, which is masculine.

57

Whether by accident or by design, Catullus does not indicate the name, or even the sex, of the person here addressed. The idea expressed is a much overworked commonplace which we shall meet again in 64.154-6, which had already been used by Homer and Euripides, and which was later to be repeated by Vergil and Ovid. In every case the person addressed is a man, and we may guess that Catullus is here reproaching not Lesbia but a friend who, like Cornificius in no. 8, has failed him when he most needed comfort.

2 **infima . . . parte**: 'from the lowest region of her belly'. For Scylla consult a reference book.

4 **in . . . casu**: 'in his utmost need'.

5 **contemptam haberes**: 'hold in contempt'. This construction, which denotes a state of mind settled and permanent, was used also by Caesar in such phrases as *uirtutem Commii perspectam habere*. **fero corde**: Supply a noun or pronoun for this descriptive ablative to qualify—'cruel-hearted one' or 'person'.

58

An exquisite idyll of passionate love, in which the poet uses all the Greek devices of antithesis and mathematically balanced structure, combined with the alliteration of which the Romans were so fond, yet without impairing the simplicity, delicacy, and airy lightness which were peculiarly his own. The poem should be compared with the lovers' dialogue in Horace, *Odes III* ix.

1 **Acmen Septimius:** The two names, carefully placed together at the very beginning, probably represent real persons. If so, the one was a Roman gentleman, the other a Greek girl, perhaps a slave. **suos amores:** 'his beloved', as usual.

3 **perdite:** 'to desperation'. **amare porro:** 'to go on loving'.

5 **quantum . . . perire:** 'as much as the most desperate of lovers'; taking up *perdite*. **pote:** See note on 32.3.

6 **Indiaque:** '*or* India'. Catullus, like Vergil in *Georgic* iv, probably means Ethiopia, which is much more *tosta* than India and where lions are much commoner.

8-9 **sinistra . . . dextra:** These words have been taken in many ways and punctuated accordingly. They probably mean 'on the left, as before on the right'. The point is that to the Romans a sneeze on the left was lucky, to the Greeks a sneeze on the right; here therefore Love is giving an auspicious signal to each of the lovers.

10 **at Acme:** 'Acme in her turn . . .'.

13-15 **sic . . . ut:** 'so . . . as'.

16 **mollibus:** 'tender' as belonging to a girl. To the Romans the marrow was the seat of the affections.

20 **mutuis animis:** 'with responsive hearts' or 'with hearts as one'. **amant amantur:** For the asyndeton cf. 27.10.

22 **Syrias Britanniasque:** 'any Syria or Britain'. In 55 B.C. Julius Caesar set out for Britain and Marcus Crassus for Syria and Parthia, providing tempting opportunities for ambitious young men. This must therefore be one of Catullus' last poems, and Dr. Macmillan is surely wrong in identifying Septimius with our poet. May we guess that the poem must have been written between the departure of Crassus for the Near East and his disastrous defeat and death, and date it accordingly?

24 'finds pleasure and delight'.

25 **ullos . . . Venerem:** We may perhaps substitute 'ever' for *ullos* and translate *homines* 'mortals' (*not* 'men' or 'human beings') and *Venerem* 'a love-match'.

59

The painful theme of the deceived husband is treated by Catullus with his customary gaiety and brightness. The leaping Priapean meter (see Appendix II) which is extremely rare in Latin, is ideally suited to the theme.

NOTES

1 **COLONIA**: not 'colony' but 'Colonia'; possibly Cologna in the neighbourhood of Verona.

2–3 **inepta . . . rediuiuis**: 'the crazy legs of your flimsy bridge propped up on old posts resurrected'.

5 **sic**: 'So' or 'On this condition'. **ex**: 'to satisfy'.

6 **Salisubsali**: 'the leaping god'; otherwise unknown.

7 **munus mihi maximi risus**: 'boon to make me laugh aloud'.

8 **uolo**: Notice the short final *o*, found occasionally in Catullus and commonly in post-Vergilian verse, e.g. Martial's familiar *non amo te, Sabidi*.

10 **uerum**: like *sed*, which occasionally means 'and'. **ut**: 'where', as in 51.3.

12 **insulsissimus est homo**: 'the fellow is an utter blockhead'. **instar**: an old indeclinable noun meaning 'image' or 'form'. With a genitive it can usually be rendered 'as big as' or 'as good as'; here 'and has less sense than . . .'.

13 **tremula**: 'rocking'. **dormientis**: *not* in agreement with *patris*!

14 **uiridissimo**: not 'greenest' but (as often) 'freshest'.

15 **delicatior**: a word, as we have seen, of very varied meaning; perhaps 'winsome' or 'skittish'.

16 **nigerrimis**: blackest, and therefore ripest and most easily damaged.

17 **uni**: Even in prose *unus*, *totus*, *ullus*, and similar words are sometimes declined like *bonus*.

18 **ex sua parte**: 'on his part'.

20 **quam . . . usquam**: *usquam* means 'anywhere', but we may translate 'as if it (the tree) did not exist at all'.

21 **talis . . . stupor**: 'In the same way that booby of mine'; abstract for concrete, somewhat as when Cicero calls Antony *pestis* or *sentina*.

22 *qui* for *quis* is normal before *sim, sis, sit*.

24 **pote**: For the lengthened final vowel see note on 35.9.

25 **supinum**: literally 'on its back'; here 'listless'.

26 **soleam**: not to be translated 'shoe', which would mislead an English reader, but 'slipper'. It was made of leather and metal and slipped over the hoof.

60

This song may have been written for a special occasion, to be sung or recited by boys and girls in alternation, or it may be merely a literary exercise. We have no reason to credit Catullus with any greater interest in religion than was felt by his conforming but sceptical contemporaries. After stating the origin of the goddess, the poet praises her as mistress of mountains, woods, and rivers; as helper of women in travail; as goddess of the crossways; and as the moon (for Diana was a conflation of several deities, originally distinct), and appeals to her to bless as in time past the people of Rome.

For the Glyconic-Pherecratean metre see Appendix II.

1 'Diana's lieges are we'.

2 **integri:** probably with both nouns—'without reproach'.

3 **Dianam:** As before, keep the word in its place.

5 **Latonia:** 'child of Latona'.

7–8 Delos was the birthplace of Diana and her brother Apollo. **deposiuit:** An archaic form used in prayers—'brought into the world'.

12 **sonantum:** The genitive plural in *-um*, scansionally convenient, is frequent in Vergil.

13–17 **tu:** The repetition of *tu* or *te*, placed first in the sentence, is common in prayers and hymns, the extreme instance being the *Te Deum laudamus*, where however this most effective order has been entirely abandoned in the English version.

dicta es: 'hast been named'. **Lucina Iuno:** 'Juno Lucina'. **Triuia:** Retain the name, which was originally an epithet of Hecate, the goddess of the crossways, identified with Diana, Phoebe, Luna, and the Greek Artemis. **notho:** *nothus* is a Greek word for 'bastard', and a regular description of the moon's 'counterfeit' light. Cf. 'moons with borrowed sheen' in Hamlet.

19–20 Belief in the moon's influence on husbandry is common.

21–24 **sis sancta:** 'be thou hallowed'—a polite command or a wish.

quocumque nomine: There are many references in both Greek and Latin to the belief that if prayers were to be answered the god must be addressed by the right name. To make sure, he was addressed by one name after another, ending up with a formula such as Catullus uses here. Cf. 13.3 *deus non bene aduocatus*. **bona ope:** Both verb and adverbial phrase belong to the vocabulary of prayer.

61

An elaborate and beautiful, if imperfect, poem, which editors have torn in two at line 40, chiefly because the first part is addressed to Malius and the rest to Allius. There being no known name of Malius, *Mali* in line 11 has been emended to *Manli* or *Malli*. But Manlius and Mallius, like Allius, are *nomina* or gentile names, and could not belong to the same person. Scholl's *mi Alli* would remove the difficulty if a parallel could be found for the ugly sixth-foot elision. Lachman's *Mani* assumes that the poet's friend was a M' Allius; but Catullus (like Cicero in his published writings) does not elsewhere address close friends by their *praenomina* or first names. Observe that in the two places where *Mani* occurs, *Alli* would not scan. If the two parts do form one whole, then we have an epistolary introduction, followed by a highly literary elegy, rounded off by an epistolary tailpiece.

A further difficulty is that the elegy is so carefully constructed, the poet going from his own love affairs through Laodamia's to Troy and the scene of his brother's death, then back through Troy and Laodamia's affairs to his own, that it seems inconsistent with his professed inability to send Manius what he wants. But Catullus only says that the time when he could write frivolous poetry is past (lines 15–17), and that absence from his library hinders him from producing the kind of learned poetry desired by his friend.

1 **QVOD:** taken up by *id* in line 9. Translate both words 'that', and place a dash before the second 'that'.

2 **epistolium:** Catullus has borrowed a Greek diminutive.

9 **tibi:** with *amicum*, not with *dicis*.

10 'The gifts of the muses and of Venus' are learned poems and love poems; both are referred to again in line 39. **hinc:** 'from me'. Notice the elision at the caesura; we have already met one in 11.6, and shall meet three more in this poem.

11 **incommoda:** 'sorrows': opposite of *commoda* 'happiness' in line 21.

12 **odisse:** not 'hate' but 'disdain' or 'disregard', the regular meaning in poetry and prose alike.

13 **quis:** Mind how you parse this word.

14 **dona beata:** 'the gifts of the happy', i.e. gifts that only happy men can give.

15 **uestis pura:** 'the white garment' or toga assumed by a Roman boy at 15 or 16 when he came of age.

16 'When my blossoming youth was keeping its joyous spring.'

17 **lusi:** See note on 23.1–2.

18 **dulcem amaritiem:** a favourite Greek oxymoron; cf. our 'bittersweet'.

19 **fraterna:** See note on 31.9.

20 **mihi:** See note on 31.5–6, and cf. line 31.

22–23 **una:** Scan.

27–30 **quod ... id:** See note on line 1. This is the standard formula for quoting from a friend's letter and replying to the quotation. **esse:** to be taken twice—'that it is a shame for Catullus to be at Verona'. The reading is doubtful. **quisquis ... nota:** Supply *est*—'every member of the better classes'. **tepefactet:** a doubtful emendation for *tepefacit*, which does not scan. The word is intentionally mild—'warms his cold limbs as best he can in his lonely bed'.

miserum: 'a misfortune'.

32 **nequeo:** Remember that *cum* with the indicative has only one meaning. Observe the dependence of the *docti poetae* on books. Alexandrian and Roman poets found much of their inspiration in the library; few drew as much inspiration from life as Catullus did.

33–34 **quod ... hoc:** perhaps similar to *quod ... id* above; but *hoc* may be ablative. **uiuimus:** not 'I am living', for Catullus is at Verona. **domus:** complement of *est* understood.

35 **carpitur:** paraphrase.

36 **capsula:** diminutive of *capsa*, a cylindrical box in which rolls were packed. **sequitur:** not 'follows' but 'accompanies'.

37–39 **nos ... quod:** Cornish well translates 'that it is due to niggardly mind or ungenerous temper that...'. Line 39 explains the *id* of 38. **utriusque:** See note on line 10. **posta est:** a compressed form common in Lucretius—'has been handed'.

41 **reticere:** transitive, as *taceo* often is, the object being the noun clause *qua ... officiis*.

44 **illius hoc studium:** 'this eager aid of his'.

46 **facite loquatur:** 'See that it says....' **anus:** 'in its old age', literally 'as an old woman'.

49 **sublimis:** an adjective, but translate adverbially 'aloft'.

51 **Amathusia:** Venus, who had a temple at Amathus in Cyprus.

52 **in quo genere:** a Ciceronian phrase—'in what matter'.

53 **tantum:** 'as hotly'. **Trinacria rupes:** 'Trinacria's rock' is Etna. The adjective was thought to mean 'with three promontories', and is frequently applied to Sicily.

54 **lympha Malia:** 'the water of Malis'. Malis was the district through which ran the Pass of Thermopylae (which took its name from the hot springs here referred to) between Mt. Oeta and the coast.

56 **tristique:** translate *-que* 'or'.

59 **qui:** Which is the antecedent? **de prona ualle:** 'down the sloping valley'.

65 **Pollucis:** 'to Pollux'. **implorata:** with *aura*.

67–69 **is:** emphatic and twice repeated. Translate each time 'he it was'. **ad quam:** The antecedent is *domum*. Translate 'he it was gave to me, he it was gave to my mistress a house in which ...'. *dominae* is an emendation: if we retain the *dominam* of the MSS, we must make it the antecedent and translate 'He it was gave me a house, he it was gave me its lady, under whose roof ...'. *communes amores* will then mean the love affairs of Catullus and Allius, not those of Catullus and Lesbia.

70–72 **se intulit:** a dignified expression used of goddesses. Perhaps 'glided'. **trito:** 'smooth'. Look up *tero*. **fulgentem plantam:** 'the sole of her shining foot' (Cornish). **arguta:** literally 'sharp'. Editors suggest 'neat', 'twinkling', 'tapping', and 'creaking'. Is there any evidence for Simpson's statement that creaking was a good omen?

74 **Protesilaeam:** 'of Protesilaus'. The first of Agamemnon's warriors to leap on to the Trojan shore, he was immediately killed. Scan the last four letters as three long syllables. **Laudamia:** more usually spelt *Laodamia*. The first five letters form a dactyl.

75 **inceptam frustra:** because Protesilaus did not live to finish it. **sanguine sacro:** 'with sacrificial blood'.

77 **Ramnusia uirgo:** 'Virgin of Ramnus', i.e. Nemesis, worshipped at Ramnus in Attica.

79 **quam:** with *desideret*—'how fiercely' (Simpson). **pium cruorem:** 'the blood that is its due'.

81–82 **ante ... quam:** Postpone the first word till you reach the second. Do the same when *post* or *prius* is separated from *quam*. **ueniens ... hiems:** 'The coming of one and then a second winter' (Cornish).

84 **posset ut:** 'that she might bear to ...'.

85 **scibant:** See note on 19.8.

86 **miles:** in apposition to the subject.

87 **tum:** 'at that time'.

89 **nefas:** 'the horror of it!'

90 **uirum et uirtutum:** Be sure to make the two nouns correspond in English—'of men and . . . deeds', or 'of heroes and . . . deeds'. In *Aeneid* i 566 Vergil imitates this line. **acerba cinis:** 'untimely pyre'. This meaning of *cinis* is frequent.

91 **quaene etiam:** Heinsius' emendation. The MS reading is metrically impossible and has no meaning. This rare idiom (found occasionally in Plautus and Horace) preserves a trace of the original interrogative force. We may translate 'the city which . . .' or start a fresh sentence 'Was it not she who . . .'.

92-94 **ei misero:** We had the same phrase in 49.4. **fratri . . . lumen:** It is surely impossible to interpret *fratri* as the dead brother and *lumen* as the light of day, since it is Catullus who is *miser*, and *tecum* must refer to someone addressed in the previous line.

97-100 **quem . . . detinet . . . terra aliena:** 'For you . . . are held by a foreign land.' **nota:** 'familiar'. **obscena:** 'sinister' or 'hateful'. **infelice:** not 'unhappy' or 'unlucky', but 'ill-omened'. **extremo solo:** 'on a far distant soil'.

101-102 **tum:** See line 87, and translate as before. **properans . . . deseruisse:** 'is said to have hastened . . . forsaking . . .'.

103 **libera:** Scan this word, and translate 'untrammelled'. **moecha:** ablative as usual with *gaudeo*.

105 Here begins a passage of 26 lines containing three elaborate similes in the Alexandrian style so greatly admired by Catullus' generation, and no doubt by the friend who had requested the poem.

107-108 **coniugium:** Here and in line 84 some editors take the word to mean 'husband', as several times in the *Aeneid*; but 'marriage' gives excellent sense. **absorbens . . . detulerat:** As in 101-102 translate the first by a verb ('engulfed'), the second by a participle. **amoris:** with *aestus*. The couplet is copied in *Aeneid* iii 421.

109 **Grai:** 'The Greeks.' Pheneus was a town near Mt. Cyllene in Arcadia.

111 **caesis . . . fodisse:** 'cutting through . . . to have dug out . . .'.

112 **audit:** 'is declared'—a grecism, found also in Horace but without the infinitive. Cf. Milton's 'Hear'st thou rather pure ethereal stream?' **falsiparens Amphitryoniades:** 'the false-fathered

NOTES 133

son of Amphitryon' (Cornish). Hercules was the son of Jupiter and Alcmena, whose husband Amphitryon became his foster-father.

113 **Stymphalia monstra:** 'the horrible creatures of Stymphalus', i.e. the man-eating birds which Eurystheus (*eri*) ordered him to destroy. Stymphalus was a district in Arcadia, Eurystheus the king of Mycenae.

115-116 After his death Hercules became a god and married Hebe, the goddess of youth.

118 **tamen indomitam:** *tamen* really goes with *docuit*, but we may translate 'though she was untamed'.

119 **confecto . . . parenti:** another phrase lifted by Vergil (*Aeneid* iv 599). Do not translate *parenti* 'parent'.

120 Modify the construction—'is the head of the late-born grandson nursed by an only daughter'. The point is that no woman could inherit a fortune, and the old man has almost given up hope of a male descendant.

121 **qui . . . inuentus:** 'a grandson who, appearing at long last as heir to the riches . . .'.

122 **nomen intulit:** 'has had his name entered'. **testatus:** deponent participle in passive sense. So *comitatus* and *pollicitus*. In each case an active form of the verb is occasionally found.

123 **impia:** The agreed translation is 'unnatural'. **derisi gentilis:** 'of the next-of-kin—a laughingstock now'. The participle is predicative—i.e. it completes the action of the verb.

124 **suscitat:** 'scares away'. **uolturium:** 'the human vulture'. The word is used for both a scavenging bird and a grasping legacy-hunter—both familiar to Catullus! **capiti:** old form of the ablative.

125-126 For convenience translate as if Catullus had written *ulla columba compare*. **compar**, a strengthened form of *par*, is here used as a noun—'mate'. **quae:** 'though she . . .'.

127 **mordenti rostro:** Avoid the alliteration 'biting beak'. Simpson suggests 'nipping bill'.

128 **multiuola:** only here in classical Latin—'amorous'.

129 **horum:** the grandfather and the dove. **uicisti:** not 'conquered' but 'surpassed', as often with *uinco* and *supero*.

130 **ut:** 'when'.

131-132 These lines are an intentional reminder of 70-71. Begin with *cui* and reverse the order (compulsory in Latin) of *nihil* and *paulo*, which modify *digna*.

135 **tamen:** Omit, or postpone to the next line.

136 **furta:** 'illicit amours'.

139 **in:** 'in the case of' or 'regarding'. **concoquit:** Lachman's emendation of the senseless and unmetrical *cotidiana*—'swallows' (literally 'digests').

140 **omniuola:** stronger than *multiuola* above—'promiscuous'. **plurima:** contrasted with *rara*—'many, many'.

141-142 **atqui:** an old emendation for the unmetrical *atque* of the MSS. Another suggestion is *at quia*. As *nec* gives no sense without a second *nec* to follow and the two lines make no sense together, it is obvious that at least one couplet has dropped out. **componier:** the archaic form of the passive infinitive, which we shall meet five times in 62, was used by Vergil also.

tolle: Whether we translate 'take up' or 'take away', we cannot determine the meaning of the line, which perhaps refers to a stock character in comedy.

143-144 'Be that as it may, she was not given to me by her father's hand, nor did she come to a house. . . .' **Assyrio:** The poets regularly name Assyria when they mean Syria, through which the products of the East were brought to Rome.

145 **mira:** Editors wish to emend to *muta* or *multa*, which would reinforce *furtiua*.

147-148 **illud:** with forward reference as often—'this'. **quem:** The antecedent is *dies*; but Catullus may have written *diem*, which would convey the same meaning in a more normal way. Cf. *plurima quae munera* in lines 153-154. **lapide candidiore:** There are many allusions to the marking of a happy day with a white stone or chalk, the verb *noto* being regularly used, or as in poem 50 the noun *nota*.

149 **quod potui:** a common expression for 'the one thing in my power'. **confectum carmine:** 'fashioned in verse'.

151 **uestrum:** See note on 18.20. *uestrum nomen* is however used by Cicero and Ovid, and may be a recognised term for 'the name of your family'.

152 **scabra rubigine:** another phrase borrowed from this poem by Vergil (*Georgic* i 495) and in a modified form by Ovid and Lucan.

153 **Themis:** Justice personified.

154 **antiquis piis:** 'the good men of an earlier day'.

155 **tua uita:** 'your beloved' (Simpson).

156-158 Both text and meaning are uncertain. The lacuna (gap) in 156 has been filled in various ways, and in 157 at least the last word is hopelessly corrupt. *domina* means 'its mistress', not 'my mistress', since Lesbia is reserved for the final couplet. *qui* stands for *is qui*; *nobis terram dedit* conceivably means 'gave me a foothold'. In 158 the hiatus makes the text improbable.

159 **mihi est**: 'who is dearer to me than my own self'. This expression, though it could hardly appear in an English love poem, is a commonplace in Latin.

62

An *epithalamium* or wedding-song, celebrating the marriage of Manlius Torquatus and Junia Aurunculeia. The bridegroom was probably L. Junius Torquatus, admired by Cicero for the excellence of his character and the high standard of his oratory. Of the bride we know nothing. The poem is Greek in metre and style, but the marriage-customs to which it contains so many references are Roman. The order of these references does not accord with the order of events, and there is nothing to suggest that the poem was to be sung or recited at the time of the wedding, or by a chorus. It is the poet's own tribute to the young people, with whom he is present in spirit. The tone is sweet, though of course Catullus had no idea of 'the marriage of true minds'.

For the Glyconic–Pherecratean metre see Appendix II, and observe how it differs from that of no. 60.

1–2 'O dweller on the hill of Helicon, Urania's child.' Helicon was the mount of Apollo and the muses in Boeotia, Urania one of the muses and mother by Apollo of Hymen or Hymenaeus, the god of marriage.

6–10 The god is attired in the same way as the bride. **suaue olentis**: see note on 36.5.

12 **concinens**: See note on 32.13.

13 **uoce tinnula**: 'with voice pitched high'. Here again the god resembles the bride.

14 **pelle**: 'beat'.

16 **Iunia Manlio**: *Iunia* may be taken here or in line 19; *Manlio* is best taken after line 20.

17–18 **qualis . . . Venus**: 'fair as Venus who dwells in Idalium, when she . . .'. Scan *uenit*. Idalium was a town in Cyprus.

19 **iudicem**: The reference is to the Judgment of Paris, when he awarded the golden apple, inscribed 'for the fairest', to the goddess who promised him the biggest reward.

20 **alite:** not 'bird' but 'omen'. We learn from Cicero that although the *auspex* no longer interpreted the flight of the birds, his presence at a marriage was still necessary. Here and in lines 44–45 *bonus* can perhaps be rendered 'gracious'.

21 Unless *uirgo* has been kept till last, it will be safest to start a new sentence here—'She is like...'.

22 **Asia:** an adjective, *myrtus* like the names of all trees being feminine. Note the long initial vowel, which shows that the reference is not to Asia either in our sense or in the usual Roman sense, but to the marshy region round the mouths of the Maeander and Cayster, where myrtles would thrive.

23 **Hamadryades:** wood-nymphs.

24 **ludicrum sibi:** 'as a plaything for themselves'.

25 Observe the unique rhythm of this line, which has aroused the suspicions of some editors.

27–28 'Hasten to leave the Thespian rock's Aonian caverns.' Thespiae was a town at the foot of Mt. Helicon in Boeotia, of which one region was called Aonia.

29–30 **super ... frigerans:** 'waters from above with cooling stream'. Aganippe was a spring.

31 **domum ... uoca:** Preserve the sound—'to her home call home's mistress'.

32 On no account translate *coniugis noui* as 'her new husband'!

34–35 Take *huc et huc* with *errans*.

36 **simul:** perhaps 'in concert'. **integrae:** Cf. 60.2.

38 **par dies:** 'a like day'. **in modum:** with *dicite*—'in measure'.

39–40 **o Hymenaee ... Hymenaee:** Quotation marks are required in English. They are provided in 117–118 below.

41 **lubentius:** Notice the first vowel, always used by Plautus and Terence—'the more readily'.

42 **citarier:** See note on 61.141 *componier*.

43 **munus:** 'office'.

44–45 'the herald of gracious Venus, the uniter of gracious love'.

46–47 **quis deus:** See note on 13.3. **amatis amantibus:** Editors who do not consider *amant amantur* in 58.20 a satisfactory parallel adopt Haupt's *anxiis est* for *est amatis*.

51 **suis:** with *inuocat* 'for his children'.

53 'loose from the girdle the folds of their robes'. *soluo*, here and in several other passages, preserves its original trisyllabic scansion.

54–55 See note on line 32—'for thee the shy bridegroom listens with eager ear'. Such spellings as *nouos* and *nouom* are correct. So too *uolt* in 174.

56 'It is thou who into the hands of the passionate young man. . . .'

58 suae: The rule that *suus* means 'belonging to the subject' is often broken where the meaning is unmistakable.

61–63 nil commodi: 'no pleasure'.

65 ausit: a frequent substitute for *audeat*. Similar forms are *faxit* and *capsit*; cf. also *sit* and *edit*.

67 dare: 'produce'. The verb is often used thus, e.g. in Horace, *Odes III* vi 47 *mox daturos progeniem uitiosiorem*. Cf. lines 72 and 177 below.

68 stirpe nitier: 'rest' or 'lean on his offspring'.

71 quae careat: 'which lacked'. The antecedent is *terra*.

77 uiden: a colloquial form of *uidesne*. Note the short *e*; also the construction with *ut* 'how' and the indicative, found also in Plautus and Vergil, the *ut* clause having perhaps been originally an exclamation independent of the *uiden*.

79 'True-born modesty holds her back' or 'tarries'. Clearly the missing lines contained a reference to the bride and some verb leading up to the subjunctive *tardet*, which is normally transitive but very occasionally intransitive.

80 'Yet listening rather to this. . . .'

86 uiderit: 'has ever seen'.

87 uario: 'many-hued'.

88 hortulo: a word used more than once by Cicero. It is clear from *diuitis* that the meaning is not 'little garden' but 'pleasure-garden'.

89 flos hyacinthinus: It is impossible to identify the flower which the Romans called *hyacinthus* and admired so greatly. Vergil's epithet *mollis* is the last which we should attach to our own hyacinth. *stare* implies that Junia was straight-backed and perhaps tall.

91 noua nupta: 'young bride'.

92–93 si iam uidetur: 'if at last it is your pleasure'. *uidetur* sometimes means 'it seems good'.

94 uiden: See note on line 77 above, and observe that here *uiden* and the following clause are grammatically quite independent.

138   POEMS OF CATULLUS

97–100 '*Your* man will not, lightly given up to a wicked paramour and pursuing shameful deeds of dishonour, seek. . . .' *tuus* is emphatic. With *deditus in* cf. *Lucretius* iii 647 *in pugnae studio dedita mens.*

102–103 **lenta:** not 'slow' but 'pliant', as regularly in Vergil. **adsitas arbores:** Vines were customarily trained on elms, as we shall read in the next poem.

104 **in:** We should write not 'into' but 'in'.

108 **candido:** The foot of the bed was no doubt made of ivory.

109–112 **quae . . . quanta gaudia quae:** 'what joys, . . . what wondrous joys, which . . .'. **uaga nocte:** Night drives her chariot across the sky—perhaps 'journeying'. **gaudeat:** 'he may enjoy'. *gaudere gaudium* (cognate accusative) is used in both verse and prose.

114 The *pinea taeda* shaken by Hymen (line 15) was imaginary: the *faces* held aloft by three young boys escorting the bride were real.

115–116 **uenire:** The final syllable is elided before the initial vowel of the next line. *modum,* on the other hand, retains the final syllable because the *i* of *io* is consonantal. Hypermeter, in hexameters a rare exception, in the present metre is quite natural, since no break is felt between the lines of a stanza. This principle (technically known as synaphea) makes possible the division of a word between two lines, of which we have had instances in lines 46 and 82. Look out for four further instances of an elided final syllable later in this poem. Observe also that the absence of a break between lines means that the long final syllable required by the metre cannot be replaced, as in other metres (and in Horace's Glyconics, which of course are heavier and slower) with a short syllable, unless lengthened by two consonants, one of them in the next line, as in 116–117 *modum io* and 162–163 *minus pulcer.* For the only apparent exception in this poem see note on 186.

119–143 These five stanzas are addressed to the bride, imagined as just arriving at her husband's house.

119–120 **ut potens et beata:** 'how rich and splendid'. Supply *est.*

121 **sine seruiat:** The combination of the imperative of *sino* with a jussive subjunctive is common in poetry from Plautus to Vergil and Horace, and appears also in *Livy II* xl 5 *sine sciam.* Cf. the similar construction after *uolo* in 179–182.

123 The only point in the whole poem where a stanza ends without pause of any kind. After lines 20 and 101 a comma sufficed; everywhere else a heavy stop is necessary.

124-126 **usque dum**: 'till the time comes when ...'. **mouens**: 'shaking'. **anilitas**: 'anility' is far too rare a word to use in English: 'old age' will do. Of course Catullus meant the *anus* herself (abstract for concrete, like *meus stupor* in 59.21). **omnia ... annuit**: 'nods assent to all for all men'. A forward tilt of the head (unintentional in the aged) signified 'Yes' to the Romans as to us.

129-130 **transfer**: This verb, like *traduco* and *traicio*, can govern two accusatives. 'Over the threshold lift with good omen your gilded feet.' She must at all costs avoid tripping. On normal occasions a lady would set her foot firmly on the *limen*, as we saw in 61.71-72. *Aureolus*, like *hortulus* in 88 above, is not a Catullan diminutive but a standard word. Cf. *lectus* and *lectulus*, which are equally common and indistinguishable in meaning. The reference here is of course to the bride's yellow slippers.

131 **rasilem ... forem**: a difficult line. Cornish gives 'enter within the polished door'; but can we extract this meaning from *subi*, which normally means 'go under, up, or up to'? Fordyce thinks that *forem* is used of the doorway and that *rasilem* refers to its worn threshold; but elsewhere *foris* denotes the door itself, and *rasilis* is applied to objects polished on purpose. Must we however assume that *limen* is the threshold of the *foris*? May it not have been nearer the highway, so that Junia would step over it, then 'go up to the polished door', then (line 136) 'look inside'?

134-136 **intus**: This adverb, which can mean 'in the inside', 'to the inside', or 'from the inside', may be taken with *aspice*, *accubans*, or *immineat*. **toro**: apparently the couch where the bridegroom reclined while awaiting the bride's approach; elsewhere *accubo* is used mostly of reclining at the dinner-table. **Tyrio**: 'crimson'. The Tyrians made dye from shellfish. **totus ... tibi**: 'is all eagerness for you'.

139 'In him no less than in you.'

140 **uritur**: Use the intransitive active in English; we do not burn flames!

141 **sed ... magis**: 'but deeper still'. *penite* (for *penitus*) is found only here.

144-145 'Loose the smooth arm, empurpled page, of the little maid.' The *praetextatus* was one of the *pueri* of line 114, who were all too young to have assumed the *toga pura* or *uirilis*.

149-150 'You honourable matrons, honourably wedded to husbands now grown old.' For *uiris* the best MSS read *unis*, which is metrically possible if interchanged with *bonae*. The meaning would then be 'wedded to one elderly man each', which seems unconvincing. Their faithfulness in marriage is sufficiently stressed by *bonae, bene,* and *senibus*. Note this special meaning of *cognitus*.

151 **collocate puellulam:** 'set the maiden in her place'—the special duty of the *pronubae*.

154 **marite:** 'married man'. This word and the following *uxor* indicate that the ceremony has reached its climax. Cf. in our own wedding ceremony the solemn words 'I pronounce that they be man and wife together'; to the Romans however marriage had little spiritual significance.

156 **ore:** not 'mouth' but 'face', as is clear from *alba* in the next line. But what are we to do with *floridulo*? The next two lines make it impossible to abandon the allusion to a flower. Cornish has 'with flowery face'; Simpson 'with a tender bloom upon her face', which is more delicate, but hardly suggests a flower.

157-158 **parthenice:** This flower has been identified with the daisy, the convolvulus, and camomile; in our ignorance we may as well content ourselves with the very meaningful translation of this (Greek) word—'maiden-flower'.
 luteum: presumably 'pink', though in line 10 it meant 'yellow'. Elsewhere it is used to describe roses, dawn, and egg-yolk! The Romans were shockingly vague in the terminology of colour; look up *purpureus* in a large dictionary.

159-160 **ita ... caelites:** an asseveration like 'So help me God'.

163 **ne remorare:** In classical Latin the use of *ne* with an imperative, of which we shall have a second instance in 63.59, is strictly confined to verse.

165-167 **bona ... iuuerit:** 'Graciously may Venus assist you.' The force of the nominative adjective is adverbial, as often in Vergil. For the tense of the verb cf. 65.18. **palam ... cupis:** 'what you desire, you desire openly'. For the second *cupis* some MSS read *capis* 'you enjoy'. **bonum:** How rarely will 'good' do as a translation of this adjective! See note on 149.

169-174 'Of the dust ... let him first cast up the sum, who ... of your joys. Joy as you will....' **ludi:** The singular after *milia* is surprising. Editors say that the noun has a collective sense; but 'thousands of sport' is as strange in Latin as in English. May we compare Vergil, *Georgic* iv 227, *sideris in numerum*, which has so troubled the commentators, and where *sideris* is not collective? or *tantum glandis* in line 81 of the same poem?

175 **date:** See note on line 67.

177-178 **indidem:** a Ciceronian word of obvious meaning. **ingenerari:** another Ciceronian word, almost always used of the male parent, as here, *uetus nomen* being the name Manlius Torquatus, which went back to very early days. Translate 'but that from the same stock they should ever be begotten',

179-182 **uolo . . . rideat:** The construction of *uolo* with jussive subjunctive is common in comedy and in Cicero's letters. See note on 121. **dulce rideat:** Cf. 36.5.

183 **semihiante:** Scan *semjiante* (four syllables). Vergil takes the same liberty with *semihominis* in *Aeneid* viii 194. The MSS have *sed mihi ante*, which is meaningless and was corrected by the great Scaliger, evidence being drawn from Apuleius, who wrote *semihiantibus labellis*. This is a good instance of the many confusions which show how poorly acquainted with classical Latin were the copyists who produced our MSS, and how great is our own debt to the patience and skill of the scholars who have provided us with a readable text of these great poems. Translate 'with half-parted lips'.

184-188 This stanza, like its predecessor, provided inspiration for Dido's appeal to her faithless lover in *Aeneid* iv 328-329—*si quis mihi paruulus aula luderet Aeneas qui te tamen ore referret*.
facile . . . omnibus: 'easily recognised by every stranger'. Words are often transposed in the MSS, and it is probable that *omnibus* and *insciis* have changed places, depriving the former of the necessary long final syllable. **pudicitiam . . . ore:** His likeness to Manlius will make it evident that there has been no other man in his mother's life.

189-193 An awkward stanza to translate. Perhaps 'May the fame that comes to him from a noble mother to make sure his descent be like the matchless renown that came from a most noble mother to abide with Telemachus, son of Penelope'. Note the care with which Catullus has kept the mother's name to the end.

195-196 **lusimus satis:** 'We have made merry long enough.' **boni coniuges:** 'gracious pair'.

197-198 'in your office constantly employ your vigorous youth'.

63

This second epithalamium differs in many ways from the first. It is much shorter; it is not uttered rhapsodically by the poet but spoken antiphonally by groups of *iuuenes* and *puellae*; it is written, not in a lively lyric measure but in hexameters, the most stately of all metres; it is far more formally constructed, symmetrical in the extreme, with constant recourse to anaphora, chiasmus, purposeful repetition, and other Greek literary devices; it does not purport to describe the wedding customs of Republican Rome; it does not name the happy couple or show any sign of having been written for a particular occasion.

The *iuuenes* and *puellae* are not boys and girls but young men and young women. A *iuuenis* was a man in his prime, and those MSS which allot the sections to the two groups describe the masculine group as *turba uirorum*. The two groups debate the rival claims of maidenhood and marriage, every argument put forward by the women being rebutted by the men (speaking the same number of lines as the women every time), until at line 58 the women retire from the contest and the men have the last word, as they had the first. Each section is rounded off with the same refrain, and the reader will have no difficulty in knowing which group is speaking, as long as he realises that the vocatives indicate the speakers, not the listeners.

1 **VESPER:** a Latin equivalent of the Greek *Hesperus*, which is used later in the poem—'Evening star', i.e. the planet Venus when it rises in the evening.

Olympo: 'in the heavens'. The local ablative appears again in line 20 *caelo*. Both words are used in the same way by Vergil, who borrows the phrase *Vesper Olympo* to end line 86 of *Eclogue* vi. In the *Iliad* the gods live on Olympus, a mountain in northern Greece; in later literature their home is in the sky, and the name Olympus takes on this new meaning.

2 **uix tandem:** 'now at last'.

3 **pinguis:** 'richly laden'.

4 **dicitur:** Here, and again in 64.11 and 66.20, a short final syllable is lengthened before *hymenaeus*. The same thing occurs more than once in Vergil, who does the same with *hyacinthus*, e.g. in *Georgic* iv 137 *tondebat hyacinthi*. As the short syllable invariably ends in a consonant, we may suspect that the *h* (representing the Greek 'rough breathing') had some consonantal force.

5 Observe that though in *Hymen* both vowels are long, in *Hymenaee* the same vowels are short. This correctly reproduces Greek usage. In the previous poem however the first syllable of *Hymen* was short.

7 **Oetaeos:** The early commentator Servius in a note on Vergil's eighth *Eclogue* tells us that Oeta was a mountain in Thessaly sacred to Hesperus, who loved the youthful Hymenaeus.

Noctifer: 'Bringer of night'—a substitute for *Vesper*. Neither name seems to have been used by any earlier writer.

NOTES

8 **uiden ... exsiluere**: See note on 62.77.

9 **uincere**: 'to surpass'—a necessary emendation of the untranslatable *uisere*. **par est**: 'it is our task'.

11 **parata**: adjectival; the verb is simply *est*. 'We have no easy victory, comrades, ready to hand' or 'as good as won'. Similarly Livy in *V* 6 has *parata uictoria*.

12 For the construction cf. 8 above. *secum ... requirunt*: 'how they silently call to mind what they have rehearsed'. This meaning of *secum* is common in Vergil.

13 **sit**: The subjunctive is generic or consecutive.

14 **penitus**: Either of the two standard meanings, 'deep down' and 'thoroughly', will give good sense. **laborant**: In a relative clause implying causation the subjunctive is normally used, and we shall find it in lines 21 and 27 of this poem; but in 66.157 we shall again meet the indicative. In only one of the four lines could scansion have been a consideration. Both moods had been used indifferently by Plautus, and the indicative is not rare in Cicero.

15 **diuisimus**: literally 'we have separated', but 'we have turned' will do.

alio ... alio: To anyone who knows the meaning of the common *alii ... alii* and of the adverbs *quo ... eo*, these words should give no trouble.

16 **amat uictoria curam**: This purposely obvious remark was twice imitated by Vergil (*Ciris* 55 and *Eclogue* iii 59).

17 **animos ... uestros**: 'at least bring your minds to bear'.

20 **quis**: See note on 13.3.

22 **retinentem**: 'clinging'.

24 **crudelius**: with *quid*.

27 **desponsa conubia**: 'contract of marriage'. The scansion of *conubium*, a word used also by Lucretius and Vergil, has been the subject of much debate, as the second syllable seems to vary in quantity. Here and in 66.141 and 158 *u* must be long. In line 57 of this poem it appears to be short. The alternative is to scan it as *conubjum*; but there is no case of this liberty elsewhere in Catullus apart from *semjiante* (62.185) which may have been the normal pronunciation. It is probable that the length of the vowel was optional. There are a number of other words with variable quantities, from *mihi*, *tibi*, and *sibi* to *Ares* in Homer and *Italus* in Vergil.

28 **uiri**: 'husbands', i.e. prospective husbands. At the *sponsio* referred to in the previous line the suitor exchanged pledges with

the young lady's father. **pepigere . . . pepigerunt:** a small scansional liberty, as natural as 'never . . . ne'er' would be in English verse. In the same way Vergil in *Eclogue* x did not hesitate to write *fleuere . . . fleuerunt*.

29 **ardor:** 'flame'.

31 **Hesperus:** 'Star of eve.' We have lost at least six lines in which the *puellae* lamented the thieving that went on when this star was shining, and one line of the answering section in which the *iuuenes* retorted that when *stella Veneris* (as Cicero calls it) appeared in its other guise as *Eous* 'Star of morn', the thieves were caught.

33 **custodia:** abstract for concrete—'the watch'.

34 **idem:** 'thou thyself'.

35 **mutato nomine:** not with *comprendis* but with *Eous* (a necessary emendation for *eosdem*). The more usual name was *Lucifer*.

39 **secretus:** 'out of sight'. **nascitur:** 'grows'—a regular meaning. **hortis:** The plural indicates a pleasure-garden, for which we previously had *hortulus*.

41 **educat:** from *educare*, a word properly used of bringing up children. Cf. the two meanings of our word 'nursery'.

42 **optauere:** the first appearance in Latin of the gnomic perfect, indicating what has often happened and still happens. It is common in later poets, and should be normally translated by an English present. This line and line 44 were closely imitated by Ovid in *Metamorphoses* iii 353 and 355.

43 **tenui:** 'sharp'. **defloruit:** a normal perfect, to be retained in English. Consult the vocabulary.

45 **dum . . . dum:** a very rare construction indeed. The second *dum* is not a conjunction but an adverb. Quintilian, commenting on this line, points out that the first *dum*=*quoad*, the second *usque eo*. We can retain the sound of the Latin by translating 'Thus it is with a maid: so long as . . . so long . . .'.

46 'When, her body defiled, she has lost the flower of her chastity.'

49 **uidua:** 'unwedded'. The metaphor of the marriage of the elm and the vine is used even in technical prose, and is very common in poetry.

51 **prono:** 'drooping'. **corpus:** 'form' or 'frame'.

52 **iam iam:** 'is on the point of . . .'. **flagellum:** a word of many meanings. Most commonly 'whip'; here 'shoot'.

NOTES 145

53 **coluere:** Here and in 55 beware of translating 'till', since in 56 the same translation must be maintained. 'Tend' and 'cherish' have been suggested.

54 **marito:** 'as her husband'. *ulmo* is of course femine; but this is no more startling than *une souris mâle* in French.

55 **par:** 'fitting'.

57 **maturo tempore:** 'in her prime'.

58 **inuisa parenti:** Cornish suggests 'distasteful to', but the regular meaning 'hateful to' is probably not too strong. Fordyce quotes two fragments of Menander, which illustrate the (to us) extraordinary attitude of the ancient father to his unmarried daughters. 'A daughter is a possession irksome to her father'; and 'A daughter is a grievous woe, hard to get rid of'. Cicero's beloved daughter Tulliola married early and repeatedly.

59 **ne pugna:** See note on 62.165.

60–61 **cui:** Supply *ei* as antecedent. Note the studied simplicity of these lines, as of so many in this poem.

62 **ex parte:** 'in part'.

64 **duobus:** The dative with *pugnare* is not found in prose and is very rare in verse. The closest parallel to the present passage is *ne cupias pugnare puellae* in *Propertius I* x 21.

64

A careful translation of a poem in the same metre by Callimachus, of which about one quarter came to light a few years ago. It is a typical Alexandrian composition, full of learned allusions and rising to no great poetic heights; but no doubt the amorous sentiments, the playful irony, and the light-hearted inversion of ordinary values, whereby the most airy trifles are made to appear of more importance than the weightiest matters, appealed to our poet's sense of humour, as did the conceit of allowing the lock of hair to do all the talking. The outline of the story is as follows. When, soon after marrying his cousin Berenice, Ptolemy Euergetes, the new king of Egypt, set out to invade Syria, the queen vowed to give a lock of her hair to the gods if he returned safely. This he did, and the lock was duly placed in a temple from which it later disappeared. Its recovery was essential, and Conon the astronomer achieved this in the most gratifying way by identifying it with a small hairlike constellation in the company of the stars.

1 **qui:** 'He who'; the antecedent is in line 7. **dispexit:** 'descried'—a favourite verb for sighting an object and discerning it clearly. The MS reading *despexit* is impossible. Do you see why?

mundi: not 'world' but 'firmament' or 'vault of heaven', the common meaning found also in 66.206. Vergil's *mundi lumina* in *Georgic* i 5–6 is perhaps a reminiscence of this passage.

3 **ut obscuretur:** an indirect question. **rapidi solis:** 'the consuming sun'. Vergil uses the same phrase, again in *Georgic* i (line 92). Elsewhere he uses the same adjective with *aestus*, *ignis*, and *Sirius* (the dog-star). We shall meet it again in Catullus. Think what *rapio* means.

5–6 A fanciful way of explaining why the moon is sometimes invisible; love calls her down from her orbit (*gyro*) to visit Endymion in a cave under Latmos, a mountain in Caria. **Triuiam:** See note on 60.13.

7 **Conon:** a famous Samian astronomer who settled in Alexandria and made a special study of eclipses (line 3).

8 **Beroniceo:** the spelling in our medieval MSS; but Catullus presumably followed that of Callimachus, whose second vowel was *e*.

10 **leuia:** Scan.

11 **tempestate:** equivalent to *tempore*, as frequently in Sallust and Livy. **nouo . . . hymenaeo:** Notice the hiatus after *nouo* and the syllable lengthened before *hymenaeo*. See note on 63.4. **auctus:** 'blest' or 'graced' as in 66.25.

12 **Assyrios:** See note on 33.143. The purpose of the raid was to rescue Ptolemy's sister, the widow of Antiochus II.

13–14 A periphrasis for 'on the morning after his wedding'. **de:** In Greek and Latin one fights 'concerning'; in English 'for' or 'over'.

15–16 **anne . . . lacrimulis:** 'or is it with feigned tear-drops that the joyous hopes of their parents are disappointed?' The diminutive *lacrimula* regularly indicates mockery.

17 **quas:** 'the drops which . . .'.

18 The hyperbaton, or alternation of parts of two clauses, is not infrequent in Greek and Latin, both dignified and colloquial. We had an example in 26.8–9. **iuerint:** The perfect subjunctive of *iuuo* is normally *iuuerim* with *u* long. Here the vowel is short, as is the rule when one vowel precedes another and is separately pronounced. Cf. the quantities of *iuerim* (from *eo*) and *ierim*, *audiuerim* and *audierim*.

20 **nouo:** Beware once more how you translate this word.

21 **luxti:** For the compressed form see note on 9.7.

22 **fratris:** The wives of the Ptolemies, if, as here, not actually their sisters, were officially described as such. The question is ironical; it must be translated as a statement with a question-mark attached.

24-25 **tibi sollicitae:** 'in your anxiety'. **toto pectore:** See note on 54.22. **mens:** 'spirit'. **excidit:** with *toto pectore*. The same verb is used similarly, but more crudely, by Horace in *Odes III* v 29-30 *nec uera uirtus, cum semel excidit, curat reponi*.

26 **a . . . uirgine:** so *a puero* 'from boyhood'; but take care with *parua*. **magnanimam:** not 'magnanimous' but 'stout-hearted'. It is a standard description of Aeneas. Cf. Greatheart in *Pilgrim's Progress*.

27 **bonum facinus:** 'glorious deed'. Note that *facinus* does not always denote a crime. The reference is to the assassination (arranged by Berenice) of her husband's cousin Demetrius, who had angered her by jilting her in favour of her mother.

28 **quod . . . alis:** The reading is doubtful and the meaning disputed. Fordyce gives 'which another, though stronger, would not venture', which is probably right, though this meaning of *fortis* is rare. **alis:** only here in extant literature; the neuter *alid* is used once by Catullus and several times by his contemporary Lucretius.

29 **mittens:** *mitto* is often used in poetry for one or other of its compounds—here and in 66.221 for *dimitto* 'part from' or 'say goodbye to'.

30 **tristi:** See note on line 21, and look up *tero*.

31 **quis:** See note on 13.3. **an quod:** 'or is it because . . .'.

32 **a caro corpore:** 'from their dear one's side'.

33 **ibi:** perhaps 'then' or 'thereupon', as in 53.6 and three times in 65.

35 **si tetulisset:** The wording is intentionally pompous—'if he contrived to return'. The reduplicated form of the verb appears again in 65.47. **haut:** This alternative for *haud* was used by Ennius and Sallust, and frequently by Plautus.

36 **Asiam:** We are told that Ptolemy conquered Asia Minor, as well as vast areas on the other side of Syria, his original target.

37 **quis:** Scan. **reddite:** 'duly given'—a regular meaning. **coetu:** a dative form used again in 66.385.

38 'I pay an old-world vow with a novel sacrifice' (Simpson).

39 Nothing could show more clearly the respect which Catullus inspired in so different a poet as Vergil than the closeness with which the latter copied this line in *Aeneid* vi 460 *inuitus, regina, tuo de litore cessi*, adding a similar oath.

41 Translate the relative clause immediately after the antecedent *caput*, and keep *digna ferat*, 'may he get what he deserves', to the end.

42 **qui:** See note on 59.22. **se postulet esse:** 'could claim to be'.

43 **maximum in oris:** 'the greatest in any land'. *ora* 'region' is not uncommon. Cicero equates it with *pars terrarum*, and we shall meet it again in 66.281.

44 **progenies Thiae:** generally taken as Thia's son, i.e. the sun; Fordyce takes it as her grandson, the north wind, and justifies *clara* by quoting Vergil (*Georgic* i yet again, line 460) *claro Aquilone*, a grecism for the wind that brings clear weather, and a good instance of the sort of hypallage of which examples will be found in the note on 65.37.

45-46 **peperere:** 'created'. **iuuentus barbara:** 'the armies of the East'. A *iuuenis* was a man of military age; *barbarus* means 'non-Greek'. **classi:** Catullus uses both forms of the ablative, as Cicero does with *nauis*.

nauit: not 'swam' but 'sailed'. The Persian fleet which attacked Greece in 480 B.C. sailed through the canal which Xerxes had caused to be dug through the neck of land joining Mt. Athos to the mainland. The mountain was of course not *euersus*, nor was it *maximus in oris*, several of its neighbours being very much loftier. Catullus is however right about the canal, unlike the sceptical Juvenal, who wrote scornfully of *uelificatus Athos, et quidquid Graecia mendax audet in historia*.

48 **ut:** used like *utinam* to introduce a wish. **Chalybon:** Greek genitive plural. So we have *Georgicon, Metamorphoseon* and *Epigrammaton*. The final syllable is long. The Chalybes were a tribe of ironworkers which Xenophon found in Pontus, and which the poets credited with the discovery of iron, or at least ironworking.

49-50 **principio institit:** 'first began'. The verb is *insisto*, not *insto*. **ferri . . . duritiem:** 'to draw iron into tough bars'.

51-52 **abiunctae . . . lugebant:** 'Sundered from them as I was a little while before, my sister locks were mourning my fate'; an awkward sentence to translate, since, as Callimachus' wording shows, *abiunctae* agrees with *mei* implied by *mea*. So Cicero wrote *meas absentis preces*, and Ovid more boldly still *nostros flentis ocellos*.

NOTES 149

52–54 **Memnonis:** son of Dawn, killed by Achilles while fighting for the Trojans. **unigena:** 'own brother' (in 66.300 'own sister').

Arsinoes Locridos: When Arsinoe, wife of Ptolemy II, died, she was identified with Venus and honoured with a temple at Zephyrium near Alexandria. Her connexion with Locris in central Greece is uncertain. Her 'winged steed' was Zephyr, the other child of Dawn. For *equos* see note on 62.54.

57 **Zephyritis:** 'the Lady of Zephyrium'. **eo:** 'to that end'.

58 'the Grecian denizen of Canopus' shores'. The only parallel to this construction is in 66.300. See note on that line. Canopus was not far from Zephyrium. The Macedonians considered themselves Greeks.

59 The obelised words are hopelessly corrupt. *inde Venus* and *diua, tibi* have been suggested; but fortunately the phrase can be omitted without spoiling the rest of the sentence, and this course should be followed in translating.

60 **Ariadnaeis:** The story of Ariadne is told at length in 66. Her crown became a constellation. **temporibus:** Be careful!

63 **cedentem:** 'as I sped'. **templa:** 'precincts'—the primitive meaning.

65 **namque:** In *Eclogue* i 14 Vergil places this conjunction one word later still. **Callisto:** a Greek dative form not found elsewhere in Latin. Callisto, daughter of Lycaon, was changed into a bear by Juno and into a constellation (Ursa Major) by Jupiter.

67 **dux:** 'leading the way'. **tandem:** The slowness of Bootes to set is often referred to by Greek and Latin poets.

68 **uix sero:** 'scarce late at night' (Cornish). Bootes only just manages to set before dawn.

70 **Tethyi:** Tethys was the wife of Ocean. Notice the short *i* of the Greek dative.

71 **pace tua:** 'by your leave'—a standard phrase. **hic:** 'at this point'. **Ramnusia uirgo:** See note on 61.77.

73 **nec si:** 'not even if'.

74 **condita quin euoluam:** 'that I may not unfold the secrets'. For the scansion see note on 62.53, and cf. line 38 of the present poem.

77–78 A difficult couplet, of which there is no certain interpretation. We may translate 'along (*una*) with which (i.e. the head), while in times past she was a virgin devoid of all perfumes, I drank many cheap ones'. This however contradicts itself, and for *unguentis, una* Morel suggested *unguentis nuptae,* (note the commas), meaning 'a married woman's perfumes'. This accords with the original Greek, and it is known that elaborate perfumes were not used till after marriage. For *quicum* see note on 41.2. Observe that *expers* here takes the ablative, as sometimes in Plautus and Sallust. In line 91 we have the usual genitive.

79 **lumine**: probably 'day' as in line 90.

80 **non prius**: with *quam* in 82. **unanimis**: See note on 3.4.

82 **libet**: Scan.

83 'your onyx jar, you who reverence the marriage laws in chaste wedlock'. With the possessive adjective as antecedent cf. 'his way that comes in triumph' (*Julius Caesar*) and 'his body and blood, who in the same night . . .' (*Book of Common Prayer*).

84 **quae**: 'the woman who'. Scan *dedit.*

85 'Ah, let the light dust drink up her wicked gifts, making them of no effect.' *irrita* is predicative.

88 **assiduus**: Keep this word in its place—'immovably'.

90 **luminibus**: See note on line 79.

91 **siris**: If this is the perfect subjunctive and not the future perfect of *sino,* the use of *non* is remarkable, though *aut non temptaris aut perfice* (quoted by Fordyce from Ovid) is similar. Both poets could have written *ne* if they were using a subjunctive; could the construction not be a variety of the 'thou shalt not . . .' command? In line 80 the negative goes closely with *prius.*

92 **affice**: 'honour me'.

93-94 The general meaning is 'If only I could get back on to the queen's head, I would gladly see all heaven in confusion'.

Hydrochoi: generally taken as a Greek dative; but the nominative is normally *Hydrochous,* and as *proximus* is sometimes a noun ('the man next door'), *proximus Hydrochoi* perhaps means 'as a near neighbour of Hydrochous'. Hydrochous (Aquarius) is of course a long way from Oarion (Orion). **fulgeret**: not from *fulgeo, fulgere,* but from *fulgero, fulgerare* (usually spelt *fulguro*), 'let it blaze'.

65

This poem is unique in its subject-matter, in the extraordinary skill with which the poet handles a most difficult metre, in its infectious excitement and breathless speed, in the vigour and colourfulness of its language, and in its sensitiveness and emotional intensity. Based no doubt on a lost Greek original, it differs completely from 'Berenice's Lock' in its feeling of utter spontaneity. It tells the story of a Greek youth who on a sudden impulse flies across the sea to Phrygia, where in order to become a priestess of Cybele he unsexes himself. When his excitement subsides and he realises that he can never resume his former activities, he bitterly repents, but finds escape impossible.

The worship of Cybele had been brought to Rome during the Second Punic War. There it was strictly controlled, since the Romans were aware of the excesses practised in Asia Minor by her votaries, excesses which remind the reader of the self-wounding of Baal's priests on Mt. Carmel, and which provided material for several Roman poets, though none seems to have told the story of Attis, who was normally regarded as a Phrygian nature-god, not a young Greek athlete.

No other Greek or Latin poem in this metre—the Galliambic —has survived. Tennyson attempted unsuccessfully to reproduce it in his 'Boadicea', of which a few lines are quoted in Appendix II, where the metrical scheme is set out. The Latin original should be read aloud, clearly and vigorously, with careful attention to natural stresses, quantities, and caesura.

2 **Phrygium:** Phrygia, in western Asia Minor, included Mt. Dindymum (line 13) and Mt. Ida (line 30). **ut:** 'as soon as'; this word is combined with *celeri*, *citato*, and *cupide* to emphasise the young man's dash to destruction. Many similar words follow in swift succession.

3 **deae:** referred to later in the poem as *Cybele*, *Cybebe* (note the length of the middle vowel), *domina Dindymena* (or *Dindymi*), *diua*, *era*, and *mater*. In Rome she was worshipped as *Magna Mater*.

4 **ibi:** 'thereupon', as in 64.33 and twice more in the present poem. **uagus animis:** 'awhirl with passion'

5 **pondera:** 'organs of manhood'.

6 **ut sensit:** 'as soon as she felt . . .'. The feminine subject is necessitated by *citata* two lines later. The ancients regarded masculinity as positive, femininity as negative, so that a man when unsexed became a woman. Hence the many feminine words that follow, e.g. *adorta*, *tremebunda*, *Gallae*, *exsecutae*, and the explanatory *notha mulier*. The last instances are in 89-90. **sine uiro:** 'without manhood'.

7 **sola:** Scan.

9 **initia:** abstract for concrete—'instruments of initiation'.

10 **terga:** plural for singular, like *sola* above and so many words in Vergil and other poets. **teneris:** Even his fingers, like his lips in line 74, have become feminine!

11-12 **Gallae:** The Galli were the priests of Cybele. **simul:** 'with me'. Cf. 23.13.

16 'endured the ravenous briny and the cruel waves of the deep'. With *truculenta pelagi* (= *truculentum pelagus*) cf. Lucretius' *pelagi severa* (and *prima uirorum*) and Vergil's *pelagi alta*; and somewhat similarly *un drôle de garçon* and 'the devil of a mess'.

17 **nimio:** 'limitless'. The word does not necessarily mean 'excessive'.

18 **erae:** with *animum*.

20 **ad domum:** This noun does not normally have a preposition, though *in domum* and *in domo* are fairly common.

21 **cymbalum:** See note on 3.6.

22 **curuo:** The Phrygian pipe was curved at the lower end, somewhat like a bass clarinet. **graue:** See note on 36.5, and cf. Vergil, *Georgic* iv 270 *graue olentia centaurea*.

23 **Maenades:** The Maenads had originally been devotees of Bacchus. **hederigerae:** one of five compound words which Catullus apparently invented for this most original poem. The others will be found in 34, 51, and 72.

24 **sacra:** substantive—'rites'. **agitant:** the standard word for 'celebrate'.

25-26 **uolitare:** literally 'fly about'; here as often 'run this way and that'.

tripudiis: wild dances (Roman, not Greek) perhaps in triple time. Cf. Horace, *Odes III* xviii 15-16 *gaudet inuisam pepulisse fossor ter pede terram*. Observe that like Vergil (and unlike journalists and broadcasters) Catullus is not afraid to use the same word more than once; we have now had *uagus* three times, *citare* four.

27-31 The first *simul* = *ut* in lines 2 and 6—'No sooner did Attis ... than the rout ...'. The second means 'at the same time'. **remugit ... recrepant:** 'give an answering roar ... an answering crash'. **animam agens:** 'gasping for breath'.

35 **lassulae:** a tender diminutive—'weary and worn'.

36 **Cerere:** 'bread'.

37 Note the two transferred epithets: *piger* and *labante* are really descriptions of the *victims* of *sopor* and *languor*. Hypallage is common in Latin poetry, particularly in the *Odes* of Horace, e.g. *pallida mors, iracunda fulmina, dente superbo*.

39 **oris aurei Sol:** The genitive is descriptive—'the golden-visaged sun' (Ellis).

40 **album:** 'bright'—a regular epithet of the sky.

41 **sonipedibus:** Originally an adjective 'with sounding feet', *sonipes* was used by Catullus, and later by Vergil, as a noun—'prancing steed'.

43 **Pasithea:** the bride of Sleep, as mentioned in the Iliad.

44 **de:** 'after'. **rapida:** 'consuming'. We have now met this word three times, in no instance meaning 'swift'.

45 **recoluit:** 'reviewed'.

46 **sine . . . foret:** Scan *quis*; 'what he had lost and where he was'.

47 **reditum tetulit:** See note on 64.35. Here perhaps 'he retraced his steps'. **rusum:** an alternative form of *rursum*.

48 **uasta:** 'awful'. Cf. 66.156 and see note on 34.3. **uisens:** Though the usual meaning is 'go and see', *uiso* can mean simply 'gaze at' or 'behold'.

49 **miseriter:** an old form; see note on 54.19.

50 **mei . . . mea:** The variation is not due to scansional convenience; *genetrix* was an established equivalent of *mater*, but *creatrix* was still felt to have verbal force calling for an objective genitive—'that gave me birth'.

53 **aput:** A doubtful spelling of *apud*. **gelida stabula:** For the vowel lengthened before two consonants in the next word see note on 35.9.

54 **earum omnia:** The unusual rhythm makes the reading seem improbable; but the line gives satisfactory sense. *furibunda* agrees with the subject.

55 **reor:** 'Must I think?' See note on 1.1.

56–57 Body and mind alike are yearning for home; hence *ipse* and *sibi* (which *pace* Fordyce is not a stopgap). **carens est:** We should expect *caret*, but *carens* is adjectival, equivalent to *uacuus*.

58 **a domo:** See note on line 20. Take *remota* with *ego*.

60 **gyminasiis:** The old Latin spelling has been restored for scansional reasons. The Romans at first found difficulty in pronouncing Greek words in which certain consonants were conjoined. These they separated by a weak vowel, which in most cases they later discarded. If *gymnasi* in line 64 is correct, Catullus has used the longer form for metrical convenience: but probably the vowel should be inserted in *gymnasi* also, giving the same rhythm as in line 70. Notice that all the nouns in line 60 are Greek, except *foro*, which stands for *agora*, a word never used in Latin.

62 'What kind of human shape is there that I have not filled?'

63 **adolescens, ephebus, puer:** According to Cicero a Roman was considered a boy till his fifteenth year, a young man till his thirtieth. *Ephebus* is a Greek word for a youth of eighteen to twenty. Attis works back from his last state to his first, then in the next four lines reviews the glories of his prime.

64 **olei:** Athletes were rubbed with oil; Simpson translates 'the oiled ring'.

65–66 **tepida:** because of the pack of admirers, who came early and bedecked the entrance *floridis corollis*.

67 **ubi esset:** 'Whenever. . . .' See note on 19.1.

68 **ferar:** 'Shall I be called . . .?'

70 **algida:** with *loca*.

71 **columinibus:** Though not a Greek word like *gymnasium*, *columen* later lost the weak vowel and became *culmen*.

73 **iam iam . . . iam iamque:** 'now, now . . . now, even now'. Both forms of the phrase are used also by Cicero and Vergil.

74 **huic labellis:** 'from her lips'. *citus* is used adverbially.

75 **geminas:** 'twin ears' is a stock phrase in Latin poetry; the epithet, though unnecessary, is no more otiose than those in such English poetic phrases as 'greene grass' and Shakespeare's 'yellow sands'. **noua:** Yet again you are warned that 'new' will not do. The meaning here is 'unexpected' or 'startling'.

76 **ibi:** as in lines 4, 42, and 48. **iuncta iuga:** 'the yoke uniting them (the two lions)', just as *iunctus pons* means 'the bridge uniting the two banks'.

77 **laeuum . . . hostem:** 'the left-hand enemy of the flock'. Why *laeuum*? Did it matter which lion? Fordyce finds *saeuum* tempting; but would any copyist change a word so obvious into one so puzzling?

78 **agedum . . . age:** 'Come now . . . come.' *ferox* is adverbial.

79 **reditum . . . ferat:** as in line 47.

81 **caede . . . cauda:** borrowed from *Iliad* xx 170–171, which also suggested the first half of line 85.

82 **mugiente fremitu:** 'with the din of your bellowing'.

83 **torosa:** 'brawny'. *torus* is anything that bulges, from a muscle to a pillow.

84 **religatque:** 'as she unties' (= *resoluens* in line 76). *minax* is adverbial.

NOTES

85 **ferus**: a noun. **rapidum**: predicative—'to fury'.

86 **uadit**: 'He strides along.' The verb implies vigorous motion. **uago**: 'ranging' (Cornish). Catullus overworks this word, as Vergil does *ingens, misceo,* and *moles.*

87 **albicantis**: 'sparkling'—probably with foam, as *litus* includes the edge of the sea. It clearly has this meaning in *Aeneid* vi 362 *nunc me fluctus habet uersantque in litore uenti.*

88 **marmora pelagi**: another reminiscence of Homer—'the marble surface of the deep'.

90 **ibi**: The meaning this time is local, not temporal.

92 **tuos**: By now such spellings should be familiar.

93 **incitatos . . . rabidos**: predicative like *rapidum* in line 85—'to frenzy . . . to madness'.

66

By far the longest of Catullus' poems, a major contribution to Latin hexameter verse, and a work from which Vergil borrowed freely, this poem has been severely criticised by some for lack of proportion and of connexion between the parts, and stoutly defended by others, notably Simpson, who points out that the same theme runs through the entire poem, unifying all its diverse elements. Recognising the corruption of his own sophisticated generation, the poet looks back to a heroic age of primitive simplicity, when in spite of their faults men could mingle with gods and do things that were great, not petty, and when wickedness was punished and goodness rewarded. The story of the desertion of Ariadne by Theseus, which makes up so much of the poem, is to the description of the marriage of Peleus and Thetis as a picture is to its frame; they are different in material, in shape, and in colour, but they are made for each other, designed by a single artist, and combine to make a beautiful and unified whole. The appreciative reader will find this picturesque, romantic, and touching poem memorable indeed. It has inspired wonderful musical settings by Monteverdi and Richard Strauss.

The 'story within a story' is familiar to all readers of *Arabian Nights' Entertainments*. The technique goes back to a much earlier time, when the usual plan was, as here, to describe a work of art. The example set by Homer in his minute description of Achilles' shield (*Iliad* xviii) was followed by many of the lesser Greek poets. Vergil was later to describe the shield of Aeneas, and in the Fourth *Georgic* to insert on a different pretext a story comparable to that of

Theseus and Ariadne, to wit that of Orpheus and Euridice—a magnificent irrelevance which is the glory of the poem.

Some notes on the peculiarities of the Catullan hexameter will be found in Appendix II.

1 **Peliaco uertice:** a phrase borrowed by Ovid. Pelion was a high mountain in Thessaly. **prognatae:** 'sprung from'—an old and dignified word, which together with *quondam* and *dicuntur* takes us back at once to the distant past.

4 **dicuntur:** Catullus, and Vergil after him, follow the Alexandrian custom of stressing their dependence on tradition. This recurs several times in the present poem. In Attis Catullus is dealing with much more recent events, and writes of them as being fully known to him.

3 **Phasidos:** a Greek genitive. Phasis was the river of Colchis, a land at the east end of the Black Sea ruled by king Aeaetes and sheltering the Golden Fleece.

4 **iuuenes:** 'warriors' or 'braves'. **Argiuae . . . pubis:** 'the flower of Argive manhood'. Borrowed by Vergil.

5 **Colchis:** ablative of *Colchi* 'the Colchians'.

6 **uada salsa:** borrowed by Vergil. **decurrere:** used by many authors to denote speeding a long distance, without any downward motion; here transitive, as several times in Cicero.

8 **quibus:** 'for them'. **summis urbibus:** Athena was of course principally associated with the Acropolis of Athens.

10 **pinea texta:** 'the pine timbers'—a phrase twice borrowed by Ovid, who makes the meaning of *texta* unmistakable.
inflexae carinae: either dative 'to the curved keel', or genitive 'of the curved hull', if Sidgwick is right in disputing the traditional interpretation of *carina*, which sometimes means 'nutshell' or 'dog's body'! For both *texta* and *inflexae* consult the vocabulary.

11 'This was the first ship to initiate in voyaging unschooled Amphitrite.' Amphitrite was the wife of Neptune, and her name stands by metonymy for the sea, as Bacchus for wine and Ceres for corn, or as in 65.36 for bread. For the meaning of *imbuit* cf. 35.17.

12 **uentosum aequor:** borrowed by Vergil in *Georgic* i 206. **proscidit:** a verb which generally means, as here, 'plough for the first time'. For the principal parts consult the vocabulary.

15 **monstrum:** 'the astonishing sight', as regularly in Vergil. **Nereides:** perhaps in loose apposition with *uultus*; but more probably *uultus* is the object, since in several authors *emergo* is transitive, as *mergo* always is.

16 **luce:** 'day'.

17 **oculis:** not 'padding'; the Greeks and Romans habitually 'saw with their eyes', 'heard with their ears', and 'threw with their hand'. See also note on 65.75.

18 **nutricum tenus:** with *exstantes*. Though prepositional in sense, *tenus* is an old noun that is placed after the word governed, which if singular is in the ablative, if plural nearly always in the genitive. *nutrix*, which elsewhere means 'wet-nurse', here means 'teat' or 'pap'.

19 **fertur:** See note on line 2.

20 For the scansion see note on 63.4.

21 **pater:** as often, Jupiter. **Pelea:** Greek accusative. In line 26 we shall have the vocative.

22–24 The apostrophe gives the maximum force to the statement of the theme of the whole poem. (If 'apostrophe' puzzles you, look the word up—and 'apostrophize' also—in your English dictionary.) **heroes:** This word, so common in Vergil, means not 'heroes' but 'demigods', persons with one divine and one human parent, such as Achilles and Aeneas. **genus:** 'offspring'. **bona:** Do *not* translate 'good'.

Line 23b is missing from the MSS, which read *mater*, no doubt because *bona matrum* is untranslatable without a noun in agreement with *bona*. *matrum* has been restored from a scholium (Latin note) on *Aeneid* v 80–81. The scholium also supplies half of the next line, which in view of Vergil's sentence (no doubt modelled on the present passage) *salue sancta parens, iterum saluete . . . umbrae paternae* can confidently be restored as *progenies, saluete, iterum saluete, bonarum!*

25 **adeo:** 'especially'. **aucte:** as in 64.11.

27 **amores:** 'his beloved', as in 5.1. As Jupiter had been warned that Thetis was destined to bear a son mightier than his father, his kindness in surrendering her was hardly disinterested!

28 **Nereine:** 'daughter of Nereus'.

29–30 **neptem:** All the Nereids were grandchildren of Tethys and Ocean, the river which according to the Greeks flowed round the great land-mass.

31 'As soon as at the appointed time these longed-for days arrived.'

34 **dona ferunt:** The reader will no doubt recall Vergil's famous *timeo Danaos et dona ferentis*.

35 **Cieros:** A town in Thessaly. The reading is doubtful. **Tempe:** Greek neuter plural. Tempe is a valley many miles north

of Phthiotis. Catullus inherited this mistake from Callimachus who should have known better; but the Roman poets made many much worse mistakes in geography.

36-37 Crannon, Larissa, and Pharsalus (where Caesar was to destroy Pompey's army) were towns in central Thessaly, Pharsalus being in the district of Pharsalia. *Pharsalia* here is of course an adjective.

38 **nemo:** placed, as regularly in prose, last in the sentence for emphasis.

39 **humilis:** 'trailing', i.e. not trained on trees. **purgatur:** 'is cleared'.

40 Notice the use of five spondees to suggest painful effort, a device used repeatedly by Vergil. **prono:** 'deep-driven' (Fordyce). The word means 'bent forwards and downwards'.

42 **infertur:** 'settles on'. **squalida:** 'dingy'—the opposite of *fulgenti* below.

43-44 **ipsius:** 'the king's'. **quacumque . . . regia:** 'as far as the sumptuous palace stretched back' (Fordyce).

45 **soliis, mensae:** Clearly in the same case, which must be dative of possession. Translate 'on'.

46 **gaudet:** Fordyce translates 'is gay', and compares Horace's *ridet argento domus*, apparently taking *regali gaza* with the verb; but the order of words strongly suggests that the ablative should be taken with *splendida*.

gaza: a Persian word already appropriated by the Greeks. Note that *z* like *x* is a double consonant.

47-49 'But the sacred marriage-couch is placed for the goddess in the middle of the palace, made from polished Indian tusk and spread with a crimson quilt steeped in the rosy dye of the shellfish.' Mortals had to be content with a *lectus genialis*; Thetis has a *puluinar*. With *Indo dente politum* cf. Vergil's *pictas abiete puppis* 'poops of painted pine'. The traditional translation of *purpura* and *purpureus* is surely wrong. Roses are not purple, and the adjective is applied elsewhere to poppies, fire, faces, cheeks, blushes, blood, and dawn, all of which can be crimson but surely not purple! But the meaning of the word is so elastic that it is even used of snow, swans, and lettuces!

50 **uestis:** 'coverlet' as often. **priscis . . . figuris:** not really a case of hypallage: the two nouns, as often in Greek, are equivalent to adjective and noun, 'human shapes'. **uariata:** 'adorned'.

51 **uirtutes:** 'valiant deeds'.

NOTES

52 **fluentisono:** only here—'torrent-voiced' (Simpson). **Diae:** Homer's name for the place where Ariadne died (*Odyssey* xi 321), and according to Callimachus the old name of Naxos.

53 **cedentem:** 'sailing away'.

classe: Editors point out that in lines 84 and 121 only one ship is mentioned and suggest that here, as in *Aeneid* vi 334 and Horace *Odes III* xi 48, *classis* means only one. But there seems no reason why in the latter passage it should not mean 'fleet', and if the former (*Lyciae ductorem classis Oronten*) is deemed inconsistent with i 113 (*unam, quae Lycios fidumque uehebat Oronten*), it may be replied that if *Lycios* means '*some* Lycians' not '*the* Lycians' there is no inconsistency; and that if there is inconsistency it is trifling compared with others in the *Aeneid*. Again, do Catullus' references to a single vessel prove that it was unaccompanied? After all, the basic meaning of *classis* is a collection or group.

54 **Ariadna:** the only form used in recognised classics. **furores:** See note on 23.11.

55 **uisit uisere:** See note on 65.48.

56 **utpote quae:** 'inasmuch as she ...' or 'no wonder, since she ...'.

57 **sola:** 'lonely', as later in the poem and also in the *Aeneid*.

59 **irrita:** predicative, as in 64.85.

60 **Minois:** 'daughter of Minos'.

62 **magnis ... undis:** the model for Vergil's *magnoque irarum fluctuat aestu* (*Aeneid* iv 532) and *magno curarum fluctuat aestu* (*Aeneid* viii 19).

63 **subtilem mitram:** 'fine-woven bonnet'.

64-65 **non contecta pectus, non iuncta papillas:** The participles agree with the subject; but it is better to disregard the grammar and render 'Her bosom not covered, her breasts not bound'. In view of Vergil's *nudus membra* and *saucia pectus* we cannot rule out the old explanation 'accusative of respect' (better 'of extent'); but it is more likely that this construction is an imitation of the Greek 'middle voice', which is passive in form but reflexive in meaning. The literal meaning will then be 'not having-covered-for-herself the bosom, not having-bound-for-herself the breasts'. So in Vergil over and over again, e.g. *caesariem effusae* and *exuuias indutus Achilli*. Most often it is a past participle that governs the noun, but sometimes a finite verb, as in *Aeneid* ii 510 *inutile ferrum cingitur*, where 'accusative of respect' is an impossible explanation. Cf. such French constructions as *il se lave le visage*. Where the same Latin construction is used of an action done to a person, not by himself but by another, a different explanation is required. See line 122.

67 **fluctus alludebant:** 'were the sport of the waves'. *fluctus* is the subject.

69–70 **uicem:** 'on account of'; like *tenus* in line 18, an old noun placed after a genitive. **ex te:** 'on you'. Apostrophes are used in Catullus for dramatic and emotional reasons, not as in Ovid for scansional convenience.

71 **externauit:** 'maddened'.

72 **Erycina:** Venus had a temple at Eryx in Sicily.

73 **illa tempestate, quo ex tempore:** 'from that time, the hour when'. We had this meaning of *tempestas* in 64.11. The *ex* would more naturally be placed before *tempestate*. **ferox:** 'bold', Livy's favourite epithet for a young man.

74 **Piraei:** the port of Athens.

75 **iniusti regis:** Minos, who, as we shall see, punished the innocent. **Gortynia templa:** 'Gortynian palace.' *templum* had already been used by Ennius with this meaning. The adjective is used loosely, the palace being not at Gortyn but at Cnossos.

76–79 The outline of this sentence is *perhibent Cecropiam solitam esse dare iuuenes et decus innuptarum Minotauro*, with *dapem* in apposition to the objects. When Androgeos (or Androgeon as here) was murdered in Attica, his father Minos demanded an annual tribute of young men and maidens to be devoured by the Minotaur, the monstrous offspring of Queen Pasiphae and a bull. The Athenians were forced by pestilence to accede to this demand, until Theseus, aided by the queen's daughter Ariadne, slew the monster, escaped from the labyrinth in which it had lived, and sailed away with the princess to Naxos.

Cecropiam: 'the land of Cecrops', legendary king of Attica.

80 **angusta moenia:** 'the little city'. Note this meaning of *moenia* (common in Vergil) and of *angusta* (applied by Caesar to *castra*). Athens was very small till Theseus brought in country-dwellers to swell the population. The little city could ill afford to lose its choicest young citizens.

82–83 **Cretam:** no preposition; like Cyprus, Crete was a 'small island'. **talia funera . . . nec funera:** 'such dead from Cecrops' land . . . yet not dead'. A grecism—they were not dead but were doomed to die.

84 **nitens:** possibly 'hurrying' but probably 'leaning on', i.e. 'borne by'.

NOTES

85 **magnanimum:** 'proud', like Caesar's *magni animi*.

86 **lumine:** 'eye', as twice later in this poem.

89 **quales myrtus:** 'like the myrtles which ...'. *myrtus* is accusative. **Eurotae flumina:** 'the streams of Eurotas', a river near Sparta.

90 **distinctos colores:** 'the varied hues'.

95 **sancte puer:** Cupid.

96 **quae:** 'thou who'. Do not translate the second *quae*. **Golgos, Idalium:** See note on 27.12.

98 **in flauo hospite:** 'for' or 'over the golden-haired guest'.

101 **monstrum:** It is difficult to find a substitute for 'monster' here, though this is likely to be misunderstood. See note on line 15.

102 **laudis:** not 'praise' but 'fame'.

103-104 'Yet not unacceptable or vain were the little gifts which she promised to the gods as she took upon herself....'

105-108 Keep the order—'for just as an oak ... or a pine ... when the ungovernable whirlwind wrenches ... is uprooted'. **Tauro:** a mountain range in south-east Asia Minor. **procul prona cadit:** 'falls outstretched and flat'. **quaeuis ... frangens:** 'smashing everything in its way'. Reading doubtful.

110 **domito ... Theseus:** 'overpowering his body Theseus laid low the savage beast'. Check the verb in the vocabulary.

111 **uanis:** 'empty'.

113 **regens uestigia filo:** 'guiding his footsteps with a thread'. So Vergil in *Aeneid* vi 30 *regens filo uestigia*.

115 Keep the order—'he should be baffled by the structure's indistinguishable windings'. Vergil was so impressed by the wording and rhythm of this line that, in addition to combining *uestigia* with *obseruare* in *Aeneid* ix 392, he twice imitated the second half of the line, writing in v 591 *irremeabilis error* and in vi 27 *inextricabilis error*.

116 **primo carmine:** not the beginning of the poem but lines 52-75.

117-118 **ut:** In 117 translate 'how'; in 118 omit. **denique:** 'even'. **consanguineae:** probably Phaedra. There were four sisters in all.

119 'who, poor woman, joyed to distraction in her daughter'. *deperdita* serves as a participle of *depereo*, which we had in 22.12. Macmillan takes *misera* as ablative.

122 **deuinctam . . . somno:** 'when her eyes were bound by sleep'. The construction is different from that of *contecta pectus* in line 64. Ariadne did not bind her own eyes: sleep bound them. This is an instance of the direct object retained with a passive verb. When an active verb governs both a direct and an indirect object, in the corresponding passive form it is normally the direct object that becomes the new subject, the indirect remaining unaltered; but occasionally it is the indirect that becomes the subject, the direct remaining unaltered. We shall have a second instance of this in line 296, and Vergil provides an outstanding instance in his *perque pedes traiectus lora tumentis*. Hector did not pierce his own feet: another man *Hectori traiecit lora per pedes tumentis*. Where an active verb governs two direct objects one can be retained, even in prose, when the verb becomes passive, e.g. *magister puerum linguam Latinam docet = a magistro puer linguam Latinam docetur*. This can of course be done in English, in which it is permissible even to change 'The queen gave a book to the boy' into 'The boy was given a book by the queen'—a thing impossible in Latin or French.

126-127 **tum conscendere, tum procurrere:** The present infinitives, following *fudisse*, represent a change in direct speech from perfect indicative to imperfect. Translate 'Now she would climb . . ., now she would run forward. . . .' **uastos:** See note on 34.3.

128 **tremuli salis aduersas in undas:** 'into the opposing waves of the quivering brine'.

131 'her face wet with tears as she uttered chill sobs'.

137 **tibi praesto:** 'in your heart', literally 'at hand for you'. . .

139-140 **haec:** emphatic—'Yet not such were the promises. . . not such the things . . .'. The dative with *iubeo* is very rare and not required here by scansion. Perhaps Catullus wrote *miseram*. *sperare iubebas* was used by Vergil to end line 325 of *Georgic* iv.

141 Copied by Vergil with small modifications in *Aeneid* iv 316.

145 **quis dum animus:** 'for so long as their mind . . .'. Observe the plural *quis* after the singular *uiri*. **apisci:** in prose *adipisci*.

146 **nil . . . nihil:** emphatic—'there is nought . . . nothing . . .'.

148 **metuere:** The gnomic perfect between *metuunt* and *curant* seems unlikely, as does *dicta metuere* 'they reverence their words'. *meminere*, suggested as an emendation, is very tempting.

149 **certe:** emphatic—'Certain it is that . . .'.

NOTES

150 **uersantem:** participle of *uersor* regarded as a deponent verb, not as the passive of *uerso*. **eripui:** Keep in its place; a word that ends a sentence and begins a line is specially emphatic. Vergil often uses this device, but it is more noteworthy in Catullus, whose stops are mostly at the ends of lines. Look for other examples in this poem.

germanum: This word usually means that both parents were the same, but Catullus accepts the Greek view that children of the same mother are virtually brothers and sisters. **creui:** from *cresco* or *cerno*? In prose *de-* is usually prefixed.

151 **dessem:** The compressed form is common in poetry and will be found in Cicero's letters. It no doubt corresponds to normal pronunciation. **supremo in tempore:** 'at the critical moment', or more poetically 'in the hour of utmost peril'.

153 A terrible fate, as the unburied were not allowed to cross the Styx. **iniacta:** normally *iniecta*. In 40.8 we had *insapiens* for *insipiens*.

154–156 For this familiar commonplace see introductory note to poem 57. Vergil in *Aeneid* vii 302 reproduces the whole of line 156 almost without alteration. Syrtis was a treacherous sandbank off the Libyan coast; Scylla and Carybdis a rock and a whirlpool (or two monsters) guarding the Straits of Messina. Be careful how you translate *uasta*.

157 **qui:** 'you who'. For the mood of *reddis* see note on 63.14.

158 **fuerant:** The tense should not be pressed.

159 **prisci:** 'old-fashioned' or 'stern'.

160 **uestras sedes:** 'your family abode'. See introductory note to poem 55.

161 A final clause.

162 **uestigia:** 'feet', a meaning not found in earlier literature.

164 **ignaris:** 'unconscious'.

166 'can neither hear the words uttered nor return an answer'— the model for Vergil's *ueras audire et reddere uoces* in *Aeneid* i 149 and *notas audire et reddere uoces* in vi 689.

168 **uacua alga:** Is 'the empty seaweed' an acceptable rendering?

170 **inuidit auris:** 'grudged a hearing'. The next two lines undoubtedly suggested Dido's *nimium felix si litora tantum numquam Dardaniae tetigissent nostra carinae*.

174 **nauita:** The uncontracted form was preferred by poets other than Horace.

in Cretam religasset funem: In 65.84 *religo* meant 'untie', and Fordyce suggests that with the present reading we must here translate 'unmoored his ship for the voyage to Crete'. Nowhere else, however, does the verb mean anything but 'tie' or 'tie up', and he suggests that we should accept the reading of one good MS *in Creta*. Even with our present reading 'tied up his cable in Crete' seems to me the only possible meaning, *Cretam* being justified by the motion implied in the whole phrase; for Ariadne means, not 'I wish he had never stayed in Crete', but 'I wish he had never arrived there'.

176 **hospes:** in apposition to *malus hic*; it must be kept to the end.

177 In this and the following lines be careful with the alternating subjunctives and indicatives.

178 **Idaeos:** There was a Mt. Ida in Crete as well as in the Troad.

179 **ponti aequor:** 'the waters of the sea'.

180 **quemne:** Disregard -*ne*; similarly with *quine* in 183.

181 **caede:** 'blood' as often in later poets.

184 **nullo colitur tecto:** *colitur* is Palmer's emendation for the very difficult *litus* of the MSS—'is occupied by no dwelling'.

186 Notice the scansion and see note on 35.9. No verb need be supplied.

188–191 **ante, prius:** Disregard these words until you reach *quam*, and then translate simply 'till'. **prodita:** 'of' or 'for my betrayal'. For *multam* consult the vocabulary. **caelestum:** We have had this compressed form already.

192 **multantes:** 'you who punish'.

193 **Eumenides:** another name for the Furies: like Euxine 'the hospitable sea', Eumenides 'the kindly ones' was a Greek euphemism for something dreaded.

194 **exspirantis:** Macmillan takes this with *pectoris* 'a dying heart'; Lewis and Short, Simpson, and Fordyce with *iras*—'the blasts of wrath'. **praeportat:** 'displays'.

196 **uae:** This interjection is usually combined with a dative; see note on 53.15. Here, as occasionally in other poets, it is used absolutely. Thus Plautus writes *uae uerbero*. **extremis:** 'inmost'.

198 **uerae nascuntur:** 'are true, and are born . . .'.

200–201 Keep the order—'with what mind . . . with such a mind . . .'.

204 **annuit inuicto numine:** 'bowed assent with sovereign nod' (Simpson and Cornish). Both Catullus and Vergil borrowed this from Homer (*Iliad* i 525).

NOTES

205 **horrida:** 'ruffled' (Simpson and Fordyce).

206 **mundus:** See note on 64.1.

207 **caeca caligine:** One of many phrases in this poem which appear also in *De Rerum Natura*. It is evident that one poet saw the work of the other, but which one we cannot say—perhaps both. The one certain fact is that Catullus died before his contemporary's masterpiece was published. There are affinities also between the works of Catullus and Lucretius and Cicero's translation of Aratus. The present phrase was borrowed by Vergil, who used it twice in the *Aeneid*.

208 **consitus:** literally 'planted', but sometimes metaphorically 'covered'.

209 **quae mandata:** Make *mandata* (which is a noun) part of the antecedent.

210 **dulcia:** a favourite word of Catullus's, and, like *tener*, one later applied to himself. Here 'welcome'. The *signa* are described in line 235.

211 **Erectheum:** 'of Erectheus', king of Athens and ancestor of Aegeus.

212 **classi:** See note on 64.45.

213 **concrederet:** a compound frequently used by Plautus and twice coupled with *commendare* by Cicero.

215 Notice the separation of the two vocatives, and cf. Aeneas' words to the ghost in *Aeneid* ii 282-283 *quibus Hector ab oris exspectate uenis?*

216 **dubios casus:** 'perilous ventures' (Simpson); 'doubtful hazards' (Cornish).

217 Theseus had been taken away in infancy by his mother, and had returned to his father only when grown up.

220 **figura:** not to be confused with its French derivative; it means 'shape'.

225 **infecta:** not the negative of *facta* but the participle of *inficio*. **uago:** That favourite word again! It implies restless motion, and like *dulcis* and *tener* (see note on line 210) is characteristic of Catullus himself.

227 **ferrugine:** The word means 'rust' or 'rust colour'; but as we saw in the case of *purpura* (see note on line 47) the Romans were extremely vague about colours. Here *obscurata* and the fact that the colour was to show that Aegeus was in mourning indicate that the colour was dark: Vergil and Ovid both describe it as *obscura*, and Vergil adds *Hibera* as a reminiscence of the present passage. But the colour could also be purple or even sea-green!

dicet: Scan this word and consult the vocabulary. Normally *in-* is prefixed.

228 **incola Itoni:** 'the dweller in Itonus', a city of central Greece where Athena had a notable temple.

230 **annuit:** The editors give 'vouchsafes', but the tense may be perfect.

232 **uigeant:** 'may remain fresh' (Macmillan).

234 **funestam uestem:** 'mourning drapery' or 'fabric'.

236 **gaudia:** 'the joyous tidings'.

238–240 **mandata, Thesea:** subject and object of *liquere*. Take *prius* with *tenentem* and supply an object 'them'. *nubes* and *cacumen* are subject and object of *linquunt* understood; the verb need not be supplied in translating.

241 **prospectum petebat:** 'was scanning the distant prospect'. The sea is three miles from the Acropolis (*arce*). This expression was reproduced by Vergil in *Aeneid* i 180.

242 'Consuming his anxious eyes in constant weeping.' *anxius* (based on *ango*) is stronger than the English derivative, but it is difficult to find a better word. *in* with the accusative is normal with *absumo*.

243 **infecti:** The MSS have *inflati* 'bellying'.

245–247 'Entering the shelter of the house, in mourning for his father's death, proud Theseus, as . . . he had brought distress on Minos' daughter, so himself incurred distress.'

249 **quae tum:** 'she meanwhile . . .'. **carinam:** obviously not the keel; if Catullus had wanted to name the part for the whole (synecdoche), he could not have made a worse choice.

250 **uoluebat:** 'was turning over' or 'revolving'—a regular meaning.

251 **parte ex alia:** 'in another part (of the tapestry)'. **florens:** 'youthful'. **Iacchus:** another name for Bacchus.

252 **Satyrorum, Silenis:** Nature-spirits, respectively youthful and aged. **Nysigenis:** 'Nysa-born.' The Greeks themselves could not locate Nysa, a town regarded as the birthplace of Bacchus.

253 **tuo amore:** Cf. 47.4 and see note on 38.2.

254–255 **quae:** Bergk's emendation of the *qui* of the MSS brings the two lines into accord with the *harum* that follows, but involves the assumption that they were preceded by a line bringing in the Maenads. May it not be that *qui* is right, and that the missing line or lines came immediately before *harum*?

NOTES 167

256–264 Both Catullus and Vergil are indebted to the Bacchae of Euripides for their descriptions of the Bacchic rites. **tecta cuspide:** The thyrsus was wreathed with ivy or vine-leaves.

259–260 A very difficult couplet. If *orgia* means 'orgies', 'revels', or 'mysteries' (the only meanings recognised by Lewis and Short) and *celebrabant* 'were celebrating' or 'thronging', what were the hollow boxes for? If, as some editors suggest, *orgia* means 'mysterious symbols', can we justify their translating *celebrabant* as 'were carrying in procession'? and can we extract any sense out of *audire*?

261–264 Fordyce draws attention to 'the adaptation of sound to sense throughout this description . . . the alliteration of *p* and *t* in 261–2, the *o* and *u* sounds of 263 and the contrasting *i*'s of 264'. It is done with restraint and skill, not in the blatant manner of the similar description in *De Rerum Natura* ii 618–20. In *Georgic* iv 64 *tinnitusque cie et matris quate cymbala circum* Vergil borrows the first two words from Catullus, the last two from Lucretius.

proceris palmis: 'with outstretched hands'. Both Caesar and Cicero use *palma* of the whole hand viewed from the palm side. **tereti . . . ciebant:** 'or were waking soft tinklings with the smooth round cymbal'. **multis:** dative of person concerned—'in many hands'. **barbara . . . cantu:** 'the oriental pipe shrilled with its fearful notes'.

267 **quae:** object of *spectando*—'all this'.

268 **decedere:** 'to give place'.

273 **leuiter . . . cachinni:** a parenthetic clause separating two clauses of which *quae* (= *undae*) is the subject. Translate *-que* 'while'. **plangore:** 'the plashing'.

275 **nantes . . . refulgent:** 'floating, gleam with the light'. *ab* denoting a cause is used frequently by the poets (especially Ovid) and occasionally by Cicero.

276 **uestibuli tecta:** Cf. line 246. As the phrase is equivalent to *uestibulum tectum*, we may legitimately transfer the epithet *regia* to the noun in the genitive.

277 **ad se quisque:** 'each to his own home'.

278 **Pelei:** an unusual genitive of *Pelion*.

279 **Chiron:** a centaur.

280 **quoscumque:** with *flores*.

281 **ora:** obviously not 'shore'. See note on 64.43.

283 **indistinctis plexos corollis:** 'twined in unsorted wreaths' (Fordyce). Chiron has brought a simple gift of wild flowers.

284 'and soothed by their pleasing scent the house smiled gladly'.

285 **Penios:** God of the river which flows through the Vale of Tempe between Ossa and Olympus. The Romans usually preferred the Latin spelling *Peneus*.

287 The two obelised words have never been convincingly emended: the rest of the line means 'leaving it (Tempe) to be filled with dances'.

288 **uacuos:** 'empty-handed'. What number and case is it? **ille:** the deictic (pointing out) use of the pronoun, as often in poetry—'lo!' **radicitus:** 'roots and all', a bold use of the adverb without any word for 'dug up'. Fordyce aptly compares Vergil's *teneram ab radice ferens cupressam* (*Georgic* i 20).

290–291 **lenta . . . Phaethontis:** 'the pliant sister of Phaethon flame-consumed'. When Phaethon drove the chariot of his father the sun too near the earth, Jupiter burnt him up with a flash of lightning and changed his weeping sisters into poplar trees. **aerea:** 'towering'.

292 **haec:** Though Caesar uses a neuter pronoun to sum up two masculine nouns and one feminine (*lepus, anser,* and *gallina*), it is rather surprising to find one summing up five nouns, all feminine. **late:** 'on every side'.

293 **fronde:** 'foliage', as often.

294 **sollerti corde:** 'astute of mind'. The heart was regarded as the seat of intelligence and cleverness, such as Prometheus had shown in giving Jupiter the warning referred to in the note on line 27.

295–297 Jupiter had chained the Titan Prometheus to a rock in the Caucasus because he had given fire to men. The story is vividly presented in Aeschylus' *Prometheus Bound*. **extenuata:** 'faded'. **silici . . . catena:** 'his limbs bound with a chain to the flinty rock'. For the construction see note on line 122.

300 **unigenam:** See note on 64.53. Catullus means Phoebe (= Artemis, Diana) who as Hecate was worshipped in Caria, where Idrieus had founded the town of Idrias. If *Idri* is correct, there must have been an alternative nominative *Idrus*, but the reading is uncertain. With the grammar of *cultricem montibus* cf. 64.58 *incola litoribus,* where as here the verbal force of the first noun enables the second to be used adverbially in the locative case. Similarly in prose we have *iter Romam*, where *iter* has the force of *ire*.

303 Gods and demigods did not recline but sat. Why the chairs were snow-white was explained in line 45.

304 'Bountifully were the tables piled with varied dainties' (Cornish).

306 **Parcae:** 'the Fates'.

307 **his:** dative of person concerned—'their'.

308 Catullus is thinking of the *toga praetexta*, which with its crimson edge surrounded the ankles of the magistrate.

310 **carpebant laborem:** 'plied their task'. *carpo*, originally 'pluck', is well suited to the task of spinning.

312–313 **supinis, prono:** 'upturned, downturned'. **formabat:** 'shaped'.

314 'twirled the spindle poised on its rounded whorl', a sort of flywheel at the bottom. *turbo*, which normally means 'whirlwind', is similarly used by Vergil in *Aeneid* vii for a spinning-top.

315 **decerpens:** 'nipping the thread' to remove excrescences. **aequabat opus:** 'smoothed the work'. *opus*, normally a task, can be used also of the finished product, e.g. one of Caesar's siegeworks.

With the deliberately jerky rhythm produced by the final monosyllable cf. Vergil's *procumbit humi bos* in *Aeneid* v.

316 **lanea morsa:** 'woolly flecks' (Simpson); 'bitten ends of wool' (Cornish). Check *morsa* in the vocabulary, and arrange your translation to show that it is antecedent to *quae*. **aridulis:** 'poor, dry'.

317 **leui:** Scan, as always.

318–319 **autem:** not to be translated 'but'. The sentence should be turned into the passive and *calathisci* kept to the end.

320 **haec:** feminine plural, as often in comedy and once at least (referring to *cohortes*) in the Gallic War. **pellentes uellera:** 'as they struck the raw wool' to loosen it before spinning. According to Varro *uellus* was so called because in early days the wool was pulled (*uello*) from the sheep's back, not shorn.

321 **talia fata:** 'such words of destiny as these'. Do not translate *fata* 'fate', as we used that word for *Parcae*. You are justified in writing '*words* of destiny', since *fatum* is really the neuter participle of *for* 'I speak' used passively (cf. *pollicitus*), and means 'the thing spoken'. **diuino:** 'prophetic', as in Juvenal's *diuina tomacula porci*—pork sausages used in divination.

322 **perfidiae:** 'falsehood'.

323–381 We have likened the whole poem to a picture within a wide frame; now we have the same thing on a much smaller scale, for the song of the Fates consists of 27 lines predicting the deeds of Achilles, enclosed within 12 lines and seven in praise of his parents, Peleus and Thetis.

323 'O thou who crownest thy splendid renown with mighty deeds of prowess.' *decus* probably refers to the reputation of Peleus' family.

324 **Emathiae:** a part of Macedonia; in poetry the whole, or Thessaly as here and in Vergil and Ovid. **Opis . . . nato:** 'most dear to the son of Ops'. Ops was the wife of Saturn and mother of Jupiter. We owe the elucidation of this line, corrupt in the MSS, to A. E. Housman. Earlier scholars had put the comma after *opis* (genitive of *opem*), making the line virtually untranslatable.

325 **luce:** 'day'. The relative clause precedes its antecedent, as does the similar clause in the next line.

326 **fata:** nominative.

327 **ducentes:** 'drawing'.

328–329 For the association of the bride with 'the auspicious star' Hesperus cf. 63.1–4, where *Vesper adest* is followed by *iam ueniet uirgo*.

330 Be careful with the subjunctive—'to flood your heart with soul-charming love' (Fordyce, who aptly quotes *Georgic* iv 516 *non ulli animum flexere hymenaei*, and Pacuvius *flexanima oratio*).

331 **languidulos:** 'languorous'.

334 **contexit:** 'has sheltered'.

336 'as the mutual affection in the heart of Thetis, in the heart of Peleus'. *Peleo* is dissyllabic like Vergil's *aureis*. In line 120 we had *praeoptarit* compressed into three syllables. The technical name for this is synezesis.

340–341 **uago:** 'far-ranging', *not* 'wandering'. **flammea:** perhaps 'flashing'. So in *Aeneid* xi 718 Camilla is described as *pernicibus ignea plantis*. Homer's favourite epithet for Achilles was 'swift of foot'.

343 **se conferet:** 'will match himself'.

345–346 **moenia:** As usual, 'city'; *uastabit* makes this plain. **periuri:** In order to marry Hippodamia Pelops had to beat her father Oenomaus in a chariot race. So he bribed his opponent's charioteer Myrtilus to lose deliberately, promising him half his kingdom. Myrtilus complied, enabling Pelops to win; but instead of giving him the promised reward Pelops murdered him.

tertius heres: Agamemnon was the son of Atreus the son of Pelops, but according to Homer Atreus was followed as king by his brother Thyestes, making Agamemnon the third inheritor of his grandfather's throne. A less likely explanation is that Catullus is using the 'inclusive reckoning', as in Roman dates, where *ante diem tertium* means 'two days before'.

350–351 The conventional signs of mourning. **putrida**: 'shrivelled', 'withered', or 'shrunken'. **uariabunt**: 'discolour' or 'bruise'.

353 **praecerpens**: 'harvesting before him'.

355 **Troiugenum**: 'sons of Troy'. The word being declined like *mensa*, the genitive plural would normally be *Troiugenarum*. The shortened form is possible only with masculine nouns, and is rare even in poetry. In 61.138 we had *caelicolum*. **infesto ferro**: 'with a foeman's steel'.

357 **unda Scamandri**: The Roman poets avoided putting a final short vowel before *sc* and similar combinations of consonants, except where a word could not otherwise be fitted into the metre. The only example in Vergil is in *Aeneid* xi 309 *ponite. spes*, where the full stop makes it easier to keep the final vowel short. Cases where the final vowel forms a long syllable with the two consonants are likewise rare. We have had two examples in this book. See note on 35.9. Scamander was one of the rivers of Troy.

359–360 It will be convenient to treat *angustans* as the verb and *tepefaciet* as the participle, and to take *caesis* with *corporum*, 'heaps of bodies' being equivalent to 'heaped bodies'. See note on line 276.

362–364 After the fall of Troy the Greeks, to secure a safe return, sacrificed Priam's daughter Polyxena to the ghost of Achilles. **denique . . . praeda**: 'The final witness shall be the prize awarded to him even in death.' **teres bustum**: 'the rounded (*not* 'round'!) barrow'.

366 **copiam**: 'power'. *copia* would in prose be followed by a genitive, not an infinitive.

367 The walls of Troy had been built by Poseidon (Neptune).

369 **quae**: The antecedent is in the adjective *Polyxenia* (=*Polyxenae*). See note on 64.83.

370 'shall bend the knee and fall forward, a headless body'; ('throw forward her body' is hardly possible in English).

372 **animi amores**: 'passions of your hearts'.

374 **iam dudum**: with *dedatur*—'even now'; some scholars take it with *cupido*—'for a long time past'.

377 An enlarged neck was regarded as proof that a marriage had been consummated.

379–380 **discordis . . . secubitu**: 'saddened by an estranged wife who sleeps alone'. **mittet**: 'cease', as often in Cicero and the poets.

382 **Pelei**: dative with *felicia*—'auspicious for Peleus'.

384 **praesentes**: 'in bodily presence'.

386 **nondum ... pietate:** 'when religion was not yet scorned'.

387 **reuisens:** 'visiting earth again'. *templo in fulgente* must be taken with line 389.

390–393 **Liber:** a common name for Bacchus. **Thyiadas:** The Thyiads were similar to the Maenads, but were specially associated with Delphi. The word forms a dactyl, *y* being treated as a consonant. **Delphi:** usually the town, here the people.

394 **Mauors:** the early form of *Mars*.

395–396 **Tritonis era:** 'the Lady of Triton', a lake or stream (locality undecided) where Athene (Minerva) was supposed to have been born. **Amarunsia uirgo:** 'the Virgin of Amarynthus' in Euboea, i.e. Artemis (Diana). Take *est hortata* together.

398 **cupido:** not 'eager' but 'greedy'.

402 'that he might be free to possess the flower of a stepmother as yet unwed'. The new wife would be stepmother to the son, who would not welcome her. The text is probably corrupt.

403 'the mother, wickedly seeking the embrace of her unsuspecting son'.

404 **diuos ... penates:** 'to sin against the gods of the household'. The best MSS read *diuos parentes* 'her sainted parents'.

405 **fanda nefanda:** 'good and evil'.

406 **iustificam:** found only here—'righteous'.

407 **dignantur:** The English form of this word is 'deign'.

408 **contingi lumine claro:** 'to be touched by the light of day', i.e. to be seen by human eyes.

APPENDIX I

The Manuscripts

MANUSCRIPTS of Catullus' poems are few, late, and so corrupt that it is evident that those who wrote them had little understanding of what they were copying from earlier manuscripts, themselves corrupt. It has taken the devoted labours of many scholars to extract sense from innumerable patches of nonsense, and to provide us with a text that we can read and enjoy. For some passages indeed there are rival reconstructions between which it is not easy to choose; but we may feel reasonably certain that for the most part the original wording has been recovered. In the text printed in this volume square brackets enclose a word or words supplied by the editor to fill a lacuna (gap) in the MSS, e.g. [meum] in 10.4; an obelus (dagger) is placed against a word too corrupt to be emended with confidence, e.g. †amitha in 10.7; and a row of dots indicates a line lost altogether, e.g. 29.4.

Not one of the surviving manuscripts dates from Roman times; and only one—*Codex Thuaneus*, or T, was written within a thousand years of the poet's death. This manuscript, alas, is an anthology of Latin poetry, and contains only one poem by Catullus (no. 63)—sixty-six lines out of more than two thousand. The earliest MSS of the complete collection go back only as far as the Fourteenth Century. These are known as *Oxoniensis* or O, *Parisinus* or G, and *Romanus* or R. They are all copies, direct or indirect, of a single MS deposited in the Tenth Century in the library of Catullus' birthplace, Verona, and known therefore as V. That MS was the archetype from which all existing copies of the poems were derived. It was itself a copy, a copy of a copy of a copy of . . .—no one can say how many copyings lay between it and the far-off original. One thing is certain: every copyist took over the mistakes of his predecessor and added new ones of his own.

At a date unknown V was lost, but not before it had been copied at least twice. O was a direct copy; G and R resemble each other in a way suggesting that they were derived from an intervening copy which introduced variations of its own, by which O was unaffected. This intervening copy, which has never been found, is known as X.

The supposed pedigree, therefore, is as follows:

```
        Original
           ┊
           ┊  ╲
           ┊   ╲T
          [V]
         ╱   ╲
        O    [X]
             ╱ ╲
            G   R
```

APPENDIX II

The Metres

1 Hendecasyllables

The normal scheme is — — — ∪ ∪ — ∪ — ∪ — ū
cui dono lepidum nouum libellum

Occasionally the first syllable is short:
meas ess(e) aliquid putare nugas

Occasionally the second is short:
arido modo pumic(e) expolitum

No other variations are admitted.

To get the rhythm into his head the student should memorise a few lines of Tennyson's experimental poem beginning
'O you chorus of indolent reviewers'

2 Iambics

(a) *Iambic Trimeters* consist of six iambic feet with a caesura, normally in the third:

∪ — | ∪ — | ∪ — | ∪ — | ∪ — | ∪ ū

phaselus ille ‖ quem uidetis hospites

The caesura is sometimes in the fourth foot:
nequisse praeterire ‖ siue palmulis

In poem 35 no variation whatever is admitted; by this means Catullus ensures the utmost lightness and speed; his lines bear little resemblance to the *Senarii* of Plautus, Terence, and Phaedrus.

(b) *Choliambics* or *Scazons* are similar to the above, with the important exception that the last syllable but one is long, giving the line a 'limping' rhythm:

∪ — | ∪ — | ∪ — | ∪ — | ∪ — | — ū

renidet ille ‖ quicquid est ubicumqu(e) est

A spondee is frequently admitted in the first or third foot, and in one instance (24.19) a tribrach in the second.

3 Glyconic–Pherecratean

The Glyconic is scanned thus: — ∪ — ∪ ∪ — ∪ —
The Pherecratean thus: — ∪ — ∪ ∪ — ū

(*a*) In the *Priapean* metre the two are combined to make one long line with caesura between them:

O Colonia quae cupis ‖ ponte ludere longo

Elision can take place at the caesura:

ne supinus eat cauaqu(e) ‖ in palude recumbat

(*b*) In the Hymn to Diana (60) each stanza consists of three Glyconics and one Pherecratean. Elision occurs between the lines:

munere assiduo ualent(em)
exercete iuuentam

(*c*) In the first Marriage Song (62) each stanza consists of four Glyconics and one Pherecratean. Elision occurs as before.

In all these metres each Glyconic must end in a long syllable, positional lengthening being secured by following a line ending in a consonant with one beginning with a consonant:

nulla quit sine te domus
liberos dare . . .

4 Sapphic stanzas consist of three longish lines and one short one:

— ∪ — — — ∪ ∪ — ∪ — ū
— ∪ ∪ — ū

ultimi flos praetereunte postquam
tactus aratr(o) est

There is often a caesura after the fifth syllable of the longer lines:

siu(e) in extremos ‖ penetrabit Indos

But as the first example shows, this is not essential. The fourth syllable is occasionally short:

pauca nuntiate meae puellae

Catullus, unlike Horace, retains the freedom and lightness of the Greek original.

5 CHORIAMBICS are used in poem 12 only. The succession of three choriambs (— ∪ ∪ —) gives the long line a peculiarly halting rhythm:

— — — ∪ ∪ — — ∪ ∪ — — ∪ ∪ — ∪ ū

iam te nil miseret, dure, tui dulcis amiculi?

6 GALLIAMBICS, used in 65 only, carry the reader relentlessly along in a tumultuous, headlong rush. The scansion admits of many variations, the commonest form being:

∪ ∪ — ∪ — ∪ — — ‖ ∪ ∪ — ∪ ∪ ∪ ∪

The caesura is always in the same place:

super alta uectus Attis ‖ celeri rate maria

The two short syllables at the beginning of either half-line can be replaced by one long:

sectam me(am) exsecutae ‖ duce me mihi comites
tibicen ubi canit Phryx ‖ curuo graue calamo

The first or second long syllable (or both) can be resolved into two short:

ego mulier eg(o) adulescens ‖ eg(o) ephebus ego puer

In one suspect line the fourth and fifth syllables are reversed:

et ear(um) omni(a) adirem ‖ furibunda latibula

In the final group of five short syllables the second and third can be replaced by one long:

aliena quae petentes ‖ uelut exsules loca

In one line only the long syllable in the second half is resolved:

dea magna dea Cybele ‖ dea domina Dindymi

As observed in the notes on this poem, the only English composition in this metre is Tennyson's Boadicea, which begins

> While about the shore of Mona those Neronian legionaries
> Burnt and broke the grove and altar of the Druid and Druidess,
> Far in the East Boädicéa, standing loftily charioted,
> Mad and maddening all that heard her in her fierce volubility,
> Girt by half the tribes of Britain, near the colony Cámulodúne,
> Yell'd and shriek'd between her daughters o'er a wild confederacy.

The most obvious fault here is the strongly stressed syllable at the beginning of each line.

7 HEXAMETERS are used for two poems (63 and 66) which together form nearly a quarter of the surviving works. The formal scheme is exactly the same as in Vergil:

$$-\ \overline{\cup\cup}\,|-\ \overline{\cup\cup}\,|-\,\|\ \overline{\cup\cup}\,|-\ \overline{\cup\cup}\,|-\ \overline{\cup\cup}\,|-\ \overline{\cup}$$

dicuntur liquidas ‖ Neptuni nasse per undas

The third-foot caesura may be replaced by caesuras in *both* second and fourth:

nutricum ‖ tenus exstantes ‖ e gurgite cano

If there is a 'weak' caesura in the third there is usually a strong also in the second and fourth:

indomitos ‖ in corde ‖ gerens ‖ Ariadna furores

But for special effect Catullus admits:

tecti frustraretur ‖ inobseruabilis error

The chief differences in rhythm between Catullan and Vergilian hexameters are these:

(*a*) The Catullan sentence fills a single line or a group of lines; the Vergilian may begin anywhere in one line and end anywhere in another. Thus in the first 100 lines of *Peleus and Thetis*, 63 end with a stop of some sort, and no complete sentence ends anywhere save at the end of a line; in the first 100 of *Aeneid* i only 45 end with a stop, and 16 sentences end within a line. This gives the variety desirable in a very long poem.

(*b*) In rather more than half Catullus' lines there is a break between the fourth and fifth feet (Bucolic Caesura). This is less common in Vergil's *Eclogues,* and much less common in his later works.

(*c*) Catullus ends one line in fifteen with two spondees; Vergil uses such endings much more sparingly. It was not a question of metrical convenience but of taste and fashion. Catullus also occasionally has as many as five spondees in a line, giving a deliberate heaviness to his heroic verse, as he gives intentional lightness to his more playful sallies.

8 ELEGIACS make up nearly one-third of Catullus' lines. Each couplet consists of a hexameter followed by a pentameter, the scheme of the latter being:

$$-\overline{\cup\cup}\,|-\overline{\cup\cup}\,|-\|-\cup\cup\,|-\cup\cup\,|\bar{\cup}$$

The Catullan couplet differs markedly from that of his successors, especially Ovid, who completely abandoned the freedom and elasticity of the Greek models. Catullus differed from Ovid in the following points, among others.

(*a*) He does not avoid elision, even at the caesura of the pentameter.

(*b*) He does not object to a succession of spondees in the hexameter; one line (10.3) consists of six.

(*c*) He does not insist that the last word of the pentameter should be noun, verb, personal pronoun, or possessive adjective, or object to its being trisyllabic, pentasyllabic, or even heptasyllabic.

(*d*) He does not put a stop at the end of every pentameter, but lets his sentence run on till it reaches its natural conclusion. He thus avoids the wearisome monotony of Ovid.

SELECT VOCABULARY

1 Common words used in their ordinary sense are not included.
2 Harder words are omitted if they have been explained in the Notes.
3 Where the basic word is given, normal derivatives are left to the reader's intelligence.
4 Quantities are marked only where mistakes might otherwise be made.
5 Genders are given only when they are not obvious from elementary rules.

abiegn-us, -a, -um: of firwood.
absor-beo, -bĕre, -bui, -ptum: swallow up.
absum-o, -ere, -psi, -ptum: take away.
acerb-us, -a, -um: bitter.
aci-es, -ei: sight.
acin-us, -i: grape.
acqui-esco, -escere, -eui, -etum: repose.
ad-imo, -imere, -emi, -emptum: take away.
ad-ipiscor, -ipisci, -eptus: obtain.
ador-ior, -iri, -tus: begin, proceed.
ad-sero, -serere, -seui, -situm: plant near.
aequal-is, -e: of the same age, contemporary.
aequor, -is (n): surface, sea.
aes, aeris (n): copper, bronze.
aeu-um, -i: age, period.
al-es, -itis: winged; a bird.
alg-a, -ae: seaweed.
algid-us, -a, -um: cold.
allocutio, -nis: address; consolation.
allu-o, -ere, -i: wash against.
aln-us, -i (f): alder.
al-o, -ere, -ui, -tum: feed, nourish.
amarac-us, -i: marjoram.
amar-us, -a, -um: bitter.
amic-io, -ire, -ui, -tum: clothe.

amn-is, -is (m): river.
ample-ctor, -cti, -xus: embrace.
anc-eps, -ipitis: two-edged.
anguin-us, -a, -um: snaky.
anhęlo (1): pant, gasp.
antenn-a, -ae: yard-arm.
antist-o, -are, -eti: surpass (+ dative).
an-us, -ūs: old woman (sometimes adjectival).
ap-er, -ri: boar.
arane-a, -ae: spider, cobweb.
aratr-um, -i: plough.
arbitri-um, -i: judgment.
ard-or, -ōris: heat.
arg-uo, -uere, -ui, -ūtum: prove (guilty).
arist-a, -ae: ear of corn.
art-us, -ūs: limb.
aru-um, -i: ploughed field.
aspernor (1): scorn.
at-er, -ra, -rum: black.
atqui: and yet.
attenuo (1): diminish.
au-deo, -dēre, -sus: dare.
aueo (2): long (aue: hail!).
au-geo, -gĕre, -xi, -ctum: make bigger.
aui-a, -ae: grandmother.
auit-us, -a, -um: a grandfather's.
aur-a, -ae: breeze.
aur-is, -is (f): ear.
auuncul-us, -i: mother's brother.
au-us, -i: grandfather.

180

SELECT VOCABULARY

bacchor (1): revel madly.
barathr-um, -i: pit, abyss.
beat-us, -a, -um: blest, happy.
bell-us, -a, -um: elegant, pretty.
bimul-us, -a, -um: two-year-old.
bomb-us, -i: booming sound.
bracchi(ol)-um, -i: arm.

cachinn-us, -i: loud laugh.
caco (1): befoul.
cacum-en, -inis (n): summit.
cael-ebs, -ibis: unpartnered.
caelit-es, -um: heavenly ones.
caen-um, -i: mud.
caesari-es, -ei: head or lock of hair.
caesi-us, -a, -um: green-eyed.
calam-us, -i: reed.
calathisc-us, -i: basket.
calig-o, -inis (f): mist, darkness.
cali-x, -cis (m): cup.
candeo (2): shine.
can-us, -a, -um: white, hoary.
caprimulg-us, -i: goatherd.
carbas-us, -i (f): canvas, sail.
carp-o, -ere, -si, -tum: pluck, criticise.
cart-a, -ae: paper, sheet; volume.
cas-us, -ūs: chance, mischance.
cateru-a, -ae: crowd.
caud-a, -ae: tail.
cau-eo, -ēre, -i, -tum: beware (of).
ce-do, -dere, -ssi, -ssum: yield, withdraw.
cerno, cernere, creui, cretum: perceive, decide.
certam-en, -inis (n): contest.
ceru-a, -ae: deer.
chore-a, -ae: dance.
ci-eo, -ēre, -ui, -tum: rouse, call forth.
cin-is, -eris (m): ashes.
cirsumsil-io, -ire: hop around.
cist-a, -ae: box.
cit-us, -a, -um: rapid.
claustr-um, -i: barrier; bolt.
clemen-s, -tis: gentle.
coaceruo (1): heap up.
coet-us, -ūs: company, gathering.
cognat-us, -a, -um: of kinsfolk.

col-o, -ere, -ui, cultum: till; inhabit; worship.
columb-us, -i: dove.
colum-en, -inis (n): height, pillar.
col-us, -i or -ūs (c): distaff.
com-a, -ae: hair, tress, foliage.
comat-us, -a, -um: leafy.
commemoro (1): mention.
commodo (1): lend.
commod-us, -a, -um: convenient.
compello (1): address.
comper-io, -ire, -ui, -tum: find out.
comple-ctor, -cti, -xus: embrace.
conf-icio, -icere, -eci, -ectum: finish; wear out.
consci-us, -a, -um: sharing a secret.
cons-ero, -erere, -eui, -itum: plant; fill.
continuo: forthwith.
conubi-um, -i: wedlock.
conu-ello, -ellere, -olsi, -olsum: tear up.
conuen-it, -ire, -it, -tum: it is agreed.
conuiu-a, -ae (m): guest.
conuiui-um, -i: banquet.
copi-a, -ae: plenty; opportunity.
cor, -dis (n): heart (cordi esse: to be pleasing).
coroll-a, -ae: garland.
corru-o, -ere, -i: fall to the ground.
cort-ex, -icis (c): bark.
coru-us, -i: raven.
crocin-us, -a, -um: saffron-hued.
cru-s, -ris (n): leg.
cult-or, -ōris (m): inhabitant; husbandman.
cultri-x, -cis (f): inhabitant.
cupid-us, -a, -um: eager, greedy.
cuspi-s, -dis (f): point.

dece-do, -dere, -ssi, -ssum: depart, make way.
decoct-or, -ōris: (fraudulent) bankrupt.
deflor-esco, -escere, -ui: drop blossoms.
deg-o, -ere, -i: spend (time).

deme-to, -tere, -ssui, -ssum: reap.
dem-o, -ere, -psi, -ptum: take away.
deprecor (1): pray that it may not happen.
der-igo, -igere, -exi, -ectum: rule (lines).
desideri-um, -i: longing, regret.
desidero (1): long for, miss.
desi-no, -nere, -i, -tum: cease.
desp-icio, -icere, -exi, -ectum: scorn.
despon-deo, -dēre, -si, -sum: promise.
despu-o, -ere, -i: spit out, reject.
destino (1): fix, determine.
deteri-or, -us: worse, inferior.
deu-ello, -ellere, -olsi, -olsum: tear off.
deuo-ueo, -uēre, -ui, -tum: dedicate.
dico (1): declare.
differt-us, -a, -um: stuffed full.
digit-us, -i: finger.
dil-igo, -igere, -exi, -ectum: love.
discidi-um, -i: separation.
disert-us, -a, -um: fluent in speech.
dōs, dōtis (f): dowry.

ebri(os)-us, -a, -um: tipsy, intoxicated.
ebur, eboris (n): ivory.
el-igo, -igere, -egi, -ectum: choose.
emul-geo, -gēre, -si, -sum: drain.
er-us, -i: master.
euhoe: euhoe or evoe. (*shout of joy*).
euiro (1): unman.
euo (1): cry 'euhoe'.
excrucio (1): torture.
ex-edo, -edere, -ēdi, -ēsum: devour.
eximi-us, -a, -um: outstanding.
expall-esco, -escere, -ui: grow pale.
exper-s, -tis: devoid.
expr-imo, -imere, -essi, -essum: translate.
exsec-o, -are, -ui, -tum: cut out.
exsil-io, -ire, -ui: spring out.

exturbo (1): tear out.
exuui-ae, -arum: spoils.

faceti-ae, -arum: witticisms.
fag-us, -i (f): beech.
fallo, fallere, fefelli, falsum: deceive, cheat.
fal-x, -cis (f): pruning-hook.
fam-es, -is (f): hunger.
famul-us, -i: servant.
fascino (1): bewitch.
fax, facis (f): torch.
fecund-us, -a, -um: fertile, rich.
fer-us, -a, -um: savage.
fet-us, -ūs: offspring.
fi-ngo, -ngere, -nxi, -ctum: invent, feign.
flagro (1): blaze.
flam-en, -inis (n): blast.
flamme-um, -i: bridal veil.
flat-us, -ūs: blast.
flau-us, -a, -um: yellow.
fl-eo, -ēre, -ēui, -ētum: weep.
flex-us, -ūs: winding.
fluito (1): float.
foc-us, -i: hearth.
fodio, fodere, fōdi, fossum: dig.
foedo (1): befoul.
for (1): speak.
for-is, -is (f): door.
foss-or, -ōris: ditcher.
frem-o, -ere, -ui, -itum: roar.
frequen-s, -tis: thronging, crowded.
fret-um, -i: strait, sea.
frig-us, -oris (n): cold.
frondat-or, -ōris: pruner.
fugo (1): rout.
ful-geo, -gēre, -si: shine.
fumo (1): smoke.
fund-us, -i: farm.
funesto (1): bring ruin upon.
fur, -tis: thief.
furcill-a, -ae: pitchfork.
furt-um, -i: theft; illicit love.
fus-us, -i: spindle.

gaz-a, -ae: treasure.
gelid-us, -a, -um: cold.
gemin-us, -a, -um: twin.
gem-o, -ere, -ui, -itum: groan.

SELECT VOCABULARY

gen-a, -ae: cheek.
gener, -i: son-in-law.
gentil-is, -is: kinsman.
gign-o, -ere, gen-ui, -itum: bring forth.
gingiu-a, -ae: gums.
gleb-a, -ae: clod.
gnat-us, -i: son.
graued-o, -inis (*f*): a cold.
gremi-um, -i: lap, bosom.
guttur, -is (*n*): throat.

haed-us, -i: kid.
haren-a, -ae: sand.
harundinos-us, -a, -um: reedy.
heder-a, -ae: ivy.
hilar-is, -e: gay.
hiulco (1): split open.
horrid-us, -a, -um: rough, savage.
hosp-es, -itis: host, guest.
hosti-a, -ae: victim.

ict-us, -ūs: stroke.
identidem: again and again.
ieiun-us, -a, -um: starved.
il-e, -is (*n*): groin.
immatur-us, -a, -um: untimely.
immit-is, -e: ungentle.
immo: nay rather.
impoten-s, -tis: headstrong, violent.
im-us, -a, -um: lowest; inmost.
inaniter: emptily.
incan-esco, -escere, -ui: grow white.
increb-esco, -escere, -ui: increase.
inept-us, -a, -um: absurd.
infest-us, -a, -um: hostile.
inficeti-ae, -arum: witlessness.
inf-icio, -icere, -eci, -ectum: dye.
infim-us, -a, -um: lowest.
infle-cto, -ctere, -xi, -ctum: bend.
ingenu-us, -a, -um: freeborn, noble.
inni-tor, -ti, -xus: press upon.
insci-us, -a, -um: unaware.
insuls-us, -a, -um: dull.
inter-eo, -ire, -ii, -itum: perish.
intor-queo, -quēre, -si, -tum: twist.
inuis-o, -ere, -i, -um: visit.

inuit-us, -a, -um: unwilling.
ira-scor, -sci, -tus: am angry.
irrit-us, -a, -um: unavailing.
irrumat-or, -ōris: filthy liver.
iugal-is, -e: nuptial.
iug-um, -i: yoke; ridge.
iuuenc-us, -i: bullock.

labell-um, -i: lip.
labo (1): totter.
lacten-s, -tis: milk-filled, swelling.
lae-do, -dere, -si, -sum: hurt.
laet-us, -a, -um: joyful.
laeu-us, -a, -um: left-hand.
lane-us, -a, -um: woollen.
lass(ul)-us, -a, -um: weary.
lateo (2): am hidden.
latibul-um, -i: hiding-place.
latro (1): bark.
laur-us, -i or -ūs (*f*): bay (tree).
laut-us, -a, -um: splendid.
leaen-a, -ae: lioness.
lect(ul)-us, -i: bed.
lēgo (1): dispatch.
len-is, -e: smooth, gentle.
lent-us, -a, -um: pliant, slow.
lepid-us, -a, -um: neat; charming.
lep-or, -ōris: charm.
let-um, -i: death.
leuam-en, -inis (*n*): solace.
lēu-is, -e: smooth.
libell-us, -i: little book.
libīd-o, -inis (*f*): desire, lust.
lībo (1): pour as a sacrifice.
librari-us, -i: bookseller.
lign-um, -i: wood, timber.
lim-es, -itis (*m*): path.
linte-um, -i: linen; sail; napkin.
liquen-s, -tis: clear.
liquid-us, -a, -um: clear, limpid.
liuid-us, -a, -um: lead-coloured, dark.
longinqu-us, -a, -um: long-lasting.
lot-um, -i: urine.
lub-et, -ēre, -uit: it pleases.
lu-ceo, -cēre, -xi: shine, dawn.
lu-geo, -gere, -xi, -ctum: mourn.
lum-en, -inis (*n*): light; eye.
lup-us, -i: wolf.
lustro (1): survey.

lūte-us, -a, -um: yellow.
lut-um, -i: mud.
lymph-a, -ae: water.
lympho (1): madden.

macul-a, -ae: spot.
madeo (2): am wet.
maer-or, -ōris: sorrow.
maest-us, -a, -um: sorrowful.
māl-um, -i: apple.
māl-us, -i (*f*): appletree; mast.
medull-a, -ae: marrow.
mellit-us, -a, -um: honey-sweet.
menstru-us, -a, -um: monthly.
mereor (2): deserve.
merso (1): overwhelm.
mess-or, -ōris: reaper.
me-tior, -tiri, -nsus: measure.
mic-a, -ae: crumb, grain.
mico (1): gleam, sparkle.
min-ax, -ācis: threatening.
mi-ngo, -ngere, -nxi, -ctum: make water.
mit-is, -e: gentle, soft.
mnemosyn-um, -i: memento.
modo: only, just now (*modo . . . modo:* now . . . now).
moech-us, -i: paramour.
moniment-um, -i: memorial.
mo-rdeo, -rdēre, -mordi, -rsum: bite.
moror (1): delay, linger.
mors-us, -ūs: bite.
mors-um, -i: bit.
mul-ceo, -cēre, -si, -sum: stroke, soothe.
mult-a, -ae: punishment.
munic-eps, -ipis: townsman.
mun-us, -eris (*n*): gift; favour; service.
muscos-us, -a, -um: mossy.

nato (1): swim, float.
naufrag-us, -i: shipwrecked person.
nebul-a, -ae: mist.
nefari-us, -a, -um: abominable.
nep-os, -ōtis: grandson, descendant.
nept-is, -is: granddaughter.
nequ-eo, -ire, -ii, -itum: cannot.

nequiquam: in vain.
nesci-us, -a, -um: ignorant.
nimirum: no doubt.
nimi-us, -a, -um: excessive, exceeding.
niteo (2): gleam.
nit-or, -ōris: gleam.
ni-tor, -ti, -sus or -xus: strive, rely on.
niue-us, -a, -um: snow-white.
not-esco, -escere, -ui: become known.
nu-bo, -bere, -psi, -ptum: wed (+ *dative*).
nug-ae, -arum: trifles.
num-en, -inis (*n*): nod; divinity.
nuto (1): nod.

obdūro (1): stand fast.
ob-eo, -ire, -ii, -itum: face.
obes-us, -a, -um: fat.
obit-us, -ūs: setting.
oblecto (1): delight.
oblī-uiscor, -uisci, -tus: forget.
ob-sum, -esse, -fui: hinder.
obt-ero, -erere, -riui, -ritum: crush.
obui-us, -a, -um: in the way.
occas-us, -ūs: setting.
occ-ido, -idere, -idi, -āsum: go down.
oleo (2): smell.
olf-acio, -acere, -eci, -actum: smell.
opac-us, -a, -um: shady.
op-em, -is (*f*): help (*opes:* wealth).
oper-io, -ire, -ui, -tum: cover.
oppr-imo, -imere, -essi, -essum: crush.
opti-ngo, -ngere, -gi: happen, befall.
opto (1): desire, choose.
orb-us, -a, -um: bereaved, bereft.
oscul-um, -i: kiss.
oti-um, -i: leisure.

paco (1): pacify, appease.
palaestr-a, -ae: wrestling-school.
palm(ul)-a, -ae: palm; victory; oarblade.
pal-us, -ūdis (*f*): swamp.

pan-do, -dere, -di, -sum: spread, open.
pang-o, -ere, pepigi, pactum: fix.
papauer, -is (n): poppy.
papill-a, -ae: nipple, breast.
pelag-us, -i (n): sea.
pell-is, -is (f): skin, hide.
penetral-is, -e: inner.
penitus: deeply, thoroughly.
penn-a, -ae: wing.
perc-ello, -ellere, -uli, -ulsum: strike down.
peregrin-us, -a, -um: foreign.
perenn-is, -e: lasting.
per-go, -gere, -rexi, -rectum: proceed.
perhibeo (2): assert.
permul-ceo, -cēre, -si, -sum: soothe.
pernici-es, -ei: destruction, ruin.
perniciter: swiftly.
pes, pedis (m): foot, 'sheet'.
petit-or, -ōris: candidate.
pig-er, -ra, -rum: slothful.
pign-us, -oris (n): pledge.
pil-us, -i: straw; whit (*literally* hair).
pi-us, -a, -um: loyal.
plan-go, -gere, -xi, -ctum: beat.
platan-us, -i (f): plane tree.
ple-cto, -ctere, -xi, -xum: weave.
plumb-um, -i: lead.
pōcul-um, -i: cup.
poll-ex, -icis (m): thumb.
pont-us, -i: sea.
porro: further, henceforth.
postmodo: shortly.
pote, potis: able.
praec-eps, -ipitis: headlong.
praedico (1): proclaim.
praefor (1): speak introductory words.
praegestio (4): desire greatly.
praes-es, -idis: guardian.
primaeu-us, -a, -um: youthful.
prisc-us, -a, -um: ancient.
probr-um, -i: lewdness; infamy.
procell-a, -ae: storm.
procer-us, -a, -um: tall; outstretched.
profan-us, -a, -um: uninitiated.

procliu-us, -a, -um: sloping.
pron-us, -a, -um: leaning forward; sloping down.
prosci-ndo, -ndere, -di, -ssum: plough for the first time.
prosil-io, -ire, -ui: leap forward.
prost-erno, -ernere, -raui, -ratum: lay low.
pro-sum, -desse, -fui: benefit (+*dative*).
pudic-us, -a, -um: chaste.
puerper-a, -ae: woman in childbirth.
pupul-a, -ae: pupil of eye.
putid-us, -a, -um: stinking.
putrid-us, -a, -um: withered.

quaeso: I beg.
quasso (1): shake violently.
qua-tio, -tere, -ssi, -ssum: shake.
qu-eo, -ire, -ii, -itum: can.
querell-a, -ae: complaint, lament.
que-ror, -ri, -stus: complain, lament.
quin: why . . . not (in a question).

rabi-es, -ei: madness.
rad-ix, -īcis (f): root.
ram-us, -i: branch.
rastr-um, -i: rake.
rat-is, -is (f): raft; ship.
reboo (1): resound.
recond-o, -ere, -idi, -itum: hide (away).
recordor (1): recollect.
redd-o, -ere, -idi, -itum: give what is due.
redimio (4): encircle.
refr-ingo, -ingere, -ēgi, -actum: break.
remigi-um, -i: (set of) oars.
rem-us, -i: oar.
renideo (2): grin.
resol-uo, -uere, -ui, -ūtum: loose.
resper-go, -gere, -si, -sum: sprinkle.
reticeo (2): keep silence (about).
re-us, -i: the accused.
ri-deo, -dēre, -si, -sum: laugh.
rix-a, -ae: quarrel.
rob-ur, -oris (n): strength, trunk.

rog-us, -i: pyre.
roscid-us, -a, -um: dewy.
rostr-um, -i: beak.
rub-er, -ra, -rum: red.
rubīg-o, -inis (*f*): rust.
ruden-s, -tis (*m*): rope, halyard.
rutil-us, -a, -um: red.

sacculus: purse.
saecl-um, -i: age, generation.
saep-io, -ire, -si, -tum: fence.
saeu-us, -a, -um: savage.
sal-io, -ire, -ui, -tum: leap, dance.
salt-us, -ūs: glade.
salue: greeting!
sap-io, -ere, -ii: have sense.
sauci-us, -a, -um: wounded.
scab-er, -ra, -rum: rough.
scabi-es, -ei: itch.
scomb-er, -ri: mackerel.
scopul-us, -i: crag.
sect-a, -ae: path.
sector (1): pursue.
secub-o, -are, -ui: lie apart.
secund-us, -a, -um: following; favourable; second.
secur-is, -is (*f*): axe.
seneo (2): spend old age.
sepel-io, -ire, -iui, sepultum: bury.
seuoco (1): call away.
sībil-us, -i: rustling sound.
sicc-us, -a, -um: dry.
sid-us, -eris (*n*): constellation.
sin-us, ūs: fold; bay; bosom.
socc-us, -i: slipper.
sodal-is, -is: comrade.
soli-um, -i: seat, throne.
sōlor (1): comfort
sol-um, -i: soil, ground
sol-uo, -uere, -ui, -ūtum: loosen; pay.
sonit-us, -ūs: sound.
sop-or, -ōris: sleep.
sosp-es, -itis: safe.
sp-erno, -ernere, -reui, -retum: scorn.
spinos-us, -a, -um: thorny.
spum-a, -ae: foam.
spurco (1): soil.
stabul-um, -i: den.
stagn-um, -i: still water, pool.

stat-uo, -uere, -ui, -ūtum: establish, decide.
sternu-o, -ere, -i: sneeze.
stimulo (1): goad.
stipendi-um, -i: tribute.
stip-es, -itis (*m*): tree-trunk.
stolid-us, -a, -um: stupid.
strid-eo, -ēre, -i: creak, screech.
strophi-um, -i: breast-band.
studi-um, -i: eagerness.
suauior (1): kiss.
suau-is, -e: pleasant, sweet.
subrep-o, -ere, -si, -tum: creep.
subselli-um, -i: bench.
sudari-um, -i: napkin.
sud-or, -ōris: sweat.
su-esco, -escere, -ēui, -ētum: grow accustomed.
sum-o, -ere, -psi, -ptum: take up, undertake.
sumptuos-us, -a, -um: costly.
supero (1): surpass.
suppernat-us, -a, -um: hamstrung.
suppl-ex, -icis: suppliant.
sur-a, -ae: calf of leg.
suspiro (1): sigh.

tāb-esco, -escere, -ui: waste away.
taceo (2): am silent.
taed-a, -ae: torch.
taedet (2): it wearies.
taet-er, -ra, -rum: loathsome.
tal-us, -i: ankle.
tegm-en, -inis (*n*): covering.
te-go, -gere, -xi, -ctum: cover.
tel-a, -ae: web.
tellū-s, -ris (*f*): land.
temp-us, -oris (*n*): time; brow.
tenebr-ae, -arum: gloom.
tenu-is, -e: thin.
tenus: as far as.
tep-or, -ōris: warmth.
tere-s, -tis: smooth, round.
tero, terere, triui, tritum: wear away.
testor (1): attest.
tex-o, -ere, -ui, -tum: weave.
thalam-us, -i: bedchamber.
thias-us, -i: band of worshippers.
tibic-en, -inis: piper.

SELECT VOCABULARY

tin-go, -gere, -xi, -ctum: dip, dye.
tinnit-us, -ūs: tinkling.
tintino (1): ring.
tollo, tollere, sustuli, sublatum: lift; carry off; destroy.
torpeo (2): am numb.
tor-queo, -quēre, -si, -tum: twist, churn.
to-rreo, -rrere, -rrui, -stum: scorch.
toru-us, -a, -um: grim.
trib-uo, -uere, -ui, -ūtum: bestow.
triui-um, -i: street-corner.
tru-x, -cis: fierce.
tueor (2): gaze at; guard.
tu-ndo, -ndere, -tudi, -nsum: pound.
turb-o, -inis (m): whirlwind; whorl.
turgidul-us, -a, -um: poor swollen.
tuss-is, -is (f): cough.
tutam-en, -inis (n): safeguard, defence.
ty(m)pan-um, -i: timbrel.

uād-o, -ere: go, rush.
uad-um, -i: shallow water; sea.
uae: alas.
ualeo (2): am well (uale: farewell).
uber, -is: fertile.
uecor-s, -dis: senseless.
ueget-us, -a, -um: vigorous.
uel-um, -i: sail.
uenor (1): hunt.
uenust-us, -a, -um: charming, tasteful.
uerber: -is (n): blow.
uerecund-us, -a, -um: modest, shy.
uereor (2): fear.

uern-us, -a, -um: of spring.
uerp-us, -i: circumcised man.
uer-ro, -rere, -ri, -sum: sweep.
uert-ex, -icis (m): peak; head.
uerum: but.
uesan-us, -a, -um: crazy.
uestigi-um, -i: footstep; foot.
uest-is, -is (f): robe; coverlet.
uetern-us, -i: lethargy.
uetul-us, -a, -um: old.
uibro (1): brandish.
uic-em, -is (f): change, turn, fortune.
uil-is, -e: cheap.
uirgat-us, -a, -um: of osiers.
uireo (2): am green, flourish.
uirgult-um, -i: thicket.
uis-o, -ere, -i: visit, gaze at.
uit-is, -is (f): vine.
uito (1): shun.
uitt-a, -ae: ribbon.
ul-ciscor, -cisci, -tus: punish.
ulm-us, -i (f): elm.
uln-a, -ae: arm.
ululo (1): howl.
umbr-a, -ae: shade.
ūm-or, -ōris: moisture.
ungu-en, -inis (n): ointment.
uocatio, -nis: invitation.
uolo (1): fly.
uōmer, -is (m): ploughshare.
uorag-o, -inis (f): abyss.
uoro (1): devour.
urban-us, -a, -um: of the city; elegant.
uro, urere, ussi, ustum: burn.
usque: all the way, all the time.
ustulo (1): burn up.
uu-a, -ae: grape.

zon(ul)-a, -ae: girdle.